Praise for *Coaching Power*

"All leaders today are expected to have coaching skills as part of their leadership repertoire. This book is a treasure trove for anyone looking to develop, improve and refine their coaching skills."

—**Jayne Opperman**
CEO, Consumer Relationships,
Lloyds Banking Group.

"*Coaching Power* redefines leadership for the modern age, offering tools and mindsets to navigate the complexities of a multi-generational, fast-paced world. With insights from experienced executive coaches, it transforms coaching into an essential leadership art that unlocks agility, adaptability, and emotional intelligence. A must-read for anyone looking to inspire and empower in today's ever-changing landscape."

—**Dr. Kirstin Ferguson**
best-selling author of *Head & Heart:
The Art of Modern Leadership*

"As businesses transform and adapt to unprecedented levels of change, this book gives the reader new ways to engage, access creative solutions and navigate uncertainty. A real game changer for leaders."

—**Christine Siemssen**
Chief Marketing & Digital Officer, Danone

"The most effective professional mentors in my life have exhibited the best qualities of a good coach: exacting, but collaborative; firm, but encouraging; confident, but humble. Rooted in decades of experience coaching thousands of leaders, Tom and Luciana have delivered an indispensable guide that transforms the concept of coaching from a leadership nicety into an essential skill for navigating the complexities of today's business landscape."

—Jay Lauf
Co-Founder and Chief Commercial Officer, Charter

"*Coaching Power* is a transformative book for leaders who are looking to incorporate a coaching style into their existing suite of skills. However, it goes beyond that—it redefines how you listen, respond, question, understand, support, and challenge. Easy to read, practical, and impactful—every leader should keep this book within arm's reach."

—Kim Morgan
Chairperson, Barefoot Coaching Ltd.

"Having an executive coach has been instrumental in my developmental and leadership journey. Sharpening my coaching skills is a key area of focus for me and I am very aware that it is a skill that is expected of me from the people I interact with and lead. This book is not just a good read; it will help you become the best coach you can be."

—Temi Ofong
Global Head of Customer Channels, HSBC

"Transformative and practical: *Coaching Power* is more than a guide—it's a transformative approach to leadership that equips you with the tools to inspire, adapt, and thrive in a fast-changing world. Coaching skills are essential in unlocking your team's—and your organization's—potential and success. This is a refreshing, pragmatic, and meaningful must-read to transform your business while inspiring your people."

—Luck Dookchitra
Vice President People & Culture, Leapsome

"More than ever, coaching skills have become a key differentiator to executive advancement. This book helps put structure around these skills in a straightforward and accessible style."

—Philip Eisenbeiss
Partner, Executive Access Ltd., Practice Leader,
Private Banking and Asset Management

"Human resources professionals are going to want to recommend this book to their people to augment their coaching skills. It is full of easy to apply coaching methods and techniques to unlock the full potential of individuals, teams, and organizations. Having directly experienced the phenomenal coaching skills of the authors, I can fully vouch for the tremendous value contained in these pages."

—P.B. Subbiah
Director, Human Resources & Administration,
Pacific Basin Shipping

COACHING POWER

Leading with Coaching to
Create Individual, Team, and
Organizational Outperformance

COACHING POWER

TOM PRESTON
LUCIANA NÚÑEZ

WILEY

Published by John Wiley & Sons, Inc., Hoboken, New Jersey.
Published simultaneously in Canada.

For general information on our other products and services or for technical support, please contact our Customer Care Department within the United States at (800) 762-2974, outside the United States at (317) 572-3993 or fax (317) 572-4002.

Wiley also publishes its books in a variety of electronic formats. Some content that appears in print may not be available in electronic formats. For more information about Wiley products, visit our website at www.wiley.com.

Library of Congress Cataloging-in-Publication Data

Names: Preston, Tom, 1962- author. | Núñez, Luciana, author.
Title: Coaching power : leading with coaching to create individual, team, and organizational outperformance / Tom Preston and Luciana Núñez.
Description: Hoboken, New Jersey : Wiley, [2025] | Includes index.
Identifiers: LCCN 2024047967 (print) | LCCN 2024047968 (ebook) | ISBN 9781394293414 (hardback) | ISBN 9781394293438 (adobe pdf) | ISBN 9781394293421 (epub)
Subjects: LCSH: Executive coaching. | Leadership. | Success in business.
Classification: LCC HD30.4 .P724 2025 (print) | LCC HD30.4 (ebook) | DDC 658.4/092—dc23/eng/20241121
LC record available at https://lccn.loc.gov/2024047967
LC ebook record available at https://lccn.loc.gov/2024047968

Cover Design: Vanessa Mendozzi
Cover Image: © Elena Pimukova/Shutterstock © Artistdesign.13/Shutterstock
Author Photos: Courtesy of the Authors
SKY10098329_021225

Tom: To Emma and Charles Preston. The two most important people in my life.

Luciana: To Leticia, Gisela, and Claude: my lights. To my family and friends: my gifts.

Contents

Preface

Tom Preston is the CEO and Luciana Núñez is the Head of the Americas of The Preston Associates, one of the world's leading Executive Coaching consultancy boutiques. Between them, Tom and Luciana have coached thousands of leaders in some of the most well-known companies of our times. Both have also been senior business leaders themselves, Tom in the world of commodities and private equity, having done CEO roles in both, and Luciana in world-class corporates doing strategic marketing and divisional CEO roles.

What they see today in their Executive Coaching work is that the ability to Lead with Coaching is now not a nice-to-have, it is an essential.

Leaders today are navigating ever more complexity that comes from every angle. We are leading across five different generations, all of whom expect different forms of leadership. The commercial and organizational landscape is fast moving and unpredictable, yet we are expected to navigate it with a deep duty of care to customers, employees, the environment, and the regulatory framework, to name just a few of our stakeholders, and still make companies sustainable and profitable.

So, we have an obligation to take "VUCA" negative and turn it into "VUCA" positive, as illustrated in the following image.

Moving from VUCA negative to VUCA positive

How exactly are we supposed to do this against the commercial troubled waters we live in and the geopolitical climate across the world which is a constant assault on our and our people's psyches?

Well, we need to be clear on our definition of collective success at any given time, we need to empower people to respond with agility to the solutions we need to find every day, and we need to motivate and engage people while supporting them, providing them with both strategic and emotional leadership in a flexible style that is accessible to the panoply of people we lead.

This requires that we adopt not just a new mindset or set of learned skills—we need to acquire a totally new way of being as leaders. And this way is called coaching. Our ability to navigate change, which is all about our future value as leaders, relies ever more on this new way of being simply because every other way is diminishing in effectiveness. Hierarchy doesn't fit any more, finding all the answers ourselves and then telling people what to do increasingly runs the risk that expiration happens before implementation. Those we lead expect multiple forms of support for the mental gymnastics they are expected to perform everyday while they too undergo psychological assault in their own lives due to the pace and extremity of change. They need to find the balance between the need to be a human being as much as a human doing.

Tom and Luciana have always believed that, whether coaching an individual 1:1, a team, or a group of people, they have a responsibility not only to be great coaches to help the people they are working with, but also to help them to develop their own coaching skills to become ever better leaders. This belief was the genesis of this book. This book will equip you with the tools, frameworks, mindset, and way of being to do that, for yourself and for the people you lead and influence.

This is a book for leaders who want to Lead Through Coaching and thereby succeed, in an ever-changing world.

1

Let Us Introduce Ourselves

Hello, it's good to meet you. Thank you for choosing to join us on our Leading Through Coaching journey. It's our privilege to be your coaches and guides. Although Executive Coaches don't often talk too much about themselves to the people they work with, we feel that you have a right to know a bit about each of us. As you will see as we explore Leading with Coaching together, understanding where people come from in terms of who they are and their life stories, what they do, how they became successful, and how they interact with others are important data points.

About Us

So, I'm Tom and here is a bit about me.

On the second day of my first job at the age of 21, I got off a plane in a country I had never heard of, in a city I had never heard of, with the mission to sell 28,000 tons of sugar stored in 50 kilo bags on two giant ships that had been stranded offshore as a result of a coup d'état in Nigeria.

The country was Togo in West Africa, the city was its capital Lome.

I sold the sugar bag by bag mostly for cash which I then gave to gold dealers who bought gold and sold it in Switzerland and then paid my company for the sugar. It was a commercial baptism by fire. It took courage, creativity, resilience, and a big dose of pragmatism. It required judgment about people and situations and the ample use of intuition.

I was totally ill-equipped and completely unprepared for the commercial jungles of West Africa. I was the son of a doctor who was brought up to believe that we are born to be in service to others.

Yet I did it. Something shifted in me during those months. I learned to navigate change, to spot opportunity, to understand others.

Over time I went on to build a very successful commodity trading business, followed by a creative private equity investment business in Asia. At that time, I came to understand that calculating internal rates of return was the easy part—the difficult part, the magical part, the part that made the difference between success and failure, was the people. And I also realized, once I discovered the power of coaching, how much better I could have been had I had a coach or had I known how to coach.

This ultimately led me to do a post graduate program in Executive Coaching and then set up The Preston Associates in 2003. We are now a leading firm that specializes in the provision of Executive Coaching services to the business elite across the world—enhancing business performance through the development of better leaders.

I have had the privilege over the past 20 years of working with senior leaders from every walk of life, in multiple geographies, navigating through the Global Financial Crisis, globalization, wars, pandemics, and fundamental societal change.

Most, if not all, of those leaders would now attest to the power of Leadership through Coaching.

I look forward to sharing with you some of this experience and how to stay ahead of change through this book.

And I'm Luciana.

I am a child of the 70s in Argentina: my mom was a lawyer from a traditional family, and my dad was a guerilla fighter, so I was probably destined to be an unusual combo from the start. Reflecting on how my origins influenced me as a leader, I realized that the common theme was that I became a successful mainstream rebel: operating mostly in traditional leadership environments in Fortune 500 global companies, but known for doing things a bit differently than the norm, which helped me create a unique track record and culture anywhere I went.

Throughout my professional career, I was very fortunate to live and lead businesses in Latin America, Europe, Asia, and the United States, working with people from incredibly different backgrounds, management styles, cultures, and worldviews. This led me to be a firm believer that regardless of the quality of your ideas, if you are not capable of truly engaging your people from within, you will not get anywhere. This led me to discover the power of coaching as the not-so-secret sauce of my leadership style, helping me throughout my 20+ years in the corporate world in managing multi-million dollar businesses, and leading teams that even to this day stay in touch and remember our time together as a highlight of our careers.

As I transitioned to full-time Executive Coaching, these same beliefs stayed true, and I am now able to multiply the impact of coaching by working with thousands of leaders across industries, from start-up founders to global executives.

In addition, after decades of being the only diversity in the room, I am personally very passionate about helping under-represented leaders make the most out of their unique insight, energy, and untapped brilliance.

I will share with you through this book the many lessons I have learned on the dos and don'ts of Leading with Coaching in organizations, big and small.

"The art of coaching is to guide the person from within."

—*Bill Gates, Co-founder of Microsoft*
and Former CEO

2

Coaching Power

Here's what we know about what makes coaching such a powerful tool today.

Even just 20 years ago it was viewed as a fad, something that wouldn't last, another form of corporate snake oil. Yet here we are today with a widely held view that it is perhaps the single most effective leadership development tool out there. It is also viewed as a prerequisite for being a servant leader, being able to create psychological safety, and the ability for people to be their authentic selves in corporate environments. It is known as a valuable skill in the worlds of stakeholder management, employee engagement, the creation of purpose, and shared definitions of success. And it is a vital part of client relationship management skills whether as a private banker, a head of sales, or even, when time allows, for doctors—to name but a few. Even the biggest names in the world of corporate consultancy now struggle to stay ahead of the change curve, especially when it comes to how to stay ahead of the game, of the competition, of innovation, and of the myriad of other challenges that exist for all corporations today.

We know that the power of coaching is derived from the concept that when we create something ourselves, when we discover solutions to problems that are completely congruent to us, then we can own these and we act with conviction. This is because they are ours, we believe in them, we are their co-creators.

Sometimes, while we have the answers deep in our subconscious, we are unable to access those answers unaided; we can be too close to our own trees to see the forest we are standing in. And that is where an objective thinking partner is so valuable, as they can ask the questions we don't see that prompt the answers within us. And when we do that, we take on the role of coach.

We find it extraordinary that nobody would ever think of putting a world class athlete onto the field or into the Olympic Games without a coach, yet they do it every day in business. Almost always, the difference between a gold medal and a bronze medal is not physical, it is mental. It is about attitude, confidence, determination, ownership, and mindset. It is often also about visualizing success and what it takes to get there; yet how often do business people or those leading people take the time to facilitate that in their people and their teams? Sadly, not often enough.

Your Job as a Coach

Some time ago, the dictionary definition of a coach was: "A coach is a vehicle that takes you from where you are to where you want to be." That probably came from the time when coaches were better known to be harnessed to horses. However, that is exactly what the job of a coach is today. Someone who helps take one or more people from where they are to where they want to be, in life, in business, in their careers, or even in their level of happiness. We are people who help others to succeed, to understand, to influence, to mitigate the unhelpful, and to amplify the traits that help ourselves and others to reach goals.

Very often today, that means enhancing our performance within an organization, both individually and collectively.

When we as leaders can help others to achieve that, when we can help people navigate change and uncertainty, when we can help people find solutions that they couldn't find on their own, we become extremely valuable. The time when expertise was the most prized asset of a leader is no longer, now it is the ability to help ourselves and others navigate change. Perhaps it was, actually, ever so. But the advent of Google, AI, and all of the technological advancements in recent years have made it clear that knowledge is becoming a commodity. Real value today resides only in our ability to react and adapt to change with agility.

Hence, the power of coaching.

Coaching Is a Key Leadership Skill for the Future

As we move into the future, leadership skills are evolving to meet the demands of a rapidly changing world. In the past, many of the competencies that were considered essential had a lot more to do with classic management: expertise in a functional area, decisiveness, directing, and having all the answers were some of the most valued aspects in a competent leader.

The skills that the future will demand of leaders are much more attuned with some of the most fundamental coaching skills that we explore in this book and define in the following sections.

Adaptability and Flexibility

Leaders need to be able to navigate uncertainty and lightning-fast changes in the business landscape, while considering the consequences and anticipating the impact. Being adaptable and flexible allows leaders to adjust strategies, make quick decisions, and pivot when necessary. According to a survey by McKinsey,[1] 94% of executives believe that agility and the ability to quickly adapt to change are critical to their organization's success. Furthermore, the World Economic Forum's Future of Jobs Report[2] lists adaptability as one of the top skills needed for the workforce, emphasizing its importance in a rapidly evolving job market.

Coaching skills help leaders to develop adaptability and flexibility by exploring a wider range of options, asking better questions, and creating thinking partnerships that are second nature to the best leaders in order to broaden and enrich perspectives.

Emotional Intelligence

Understanding and regulating emotions is core to effective leadership. Thanks to the extensive work done by Daniel Goleman in this area, we know that emotional intelligence (EI) helps leaders build strong relationships based on trust, communicate effectively across the board, and navigate conflicts with empathy and understanding. According to a report by Gallup, teams led by managers with high emotional intelligence have 50% higher levels of engagement compared to teams with low EQ leaders.[3]

Coaching skills help leaders gain self-awareness through self-reflection, and equip leaders to put themselves in the shoes of other people by inquiring from a place of curiosity to understand what's truly important to them and find common ground.

Collaboration and Team Building

The times of the "hero leader" are over. The future of work is increasingly collaborative, with teams working across geographies and disciplines, and often assembling for ad hoc projects and then disbanding just as soon as they complete their mission. Leaders will need to excel at building and managing diverse teams, fostering collaboration, and creating an inclusive culture where everyone feels valued and empowered to contribute. This is not only a nice to have, but a proven driver of performance: a recent Gallup study[4] found that teams with high levels of collaboration have 21% higher profitability and performance versus industry averages.

Team coaching is a highly specific skill that leaders need to master in order to get teams through the different stages (from forming to norming, storming, and performing) much faster than before, to help accelerate the curve to get to peak performance.

Visionary Leadership

Having a clear vision for the future and the ability to inspire others to follow that vision is key to engage teams at all levels. The best visionary leaders communicate a compelling purpose and motivate their teams to achieve ambitious goals by clearly articulating what's in it for them. Visionary leaders who are able to rally an organization behind their vision ultimately drive superior performance: According to a Deloitte study[5] companies with a clear vision statement, often developed by visionary leaders, are 70% more likely to outperform their peers in terms of revenue growth. Visionary leaders who prioritize growth and innovation are significantly more likely to outperform their competitors, reporting up to 7% higher stock price appreciation over three years compared to industry averages.

In this book we explore how the "Emotional Leadership" coaching framework can help you articulate a compelling vision, provide context for what matters, establish what's in it for the organization at large and for the individuals, and set the scene for defining and tracking success, which is key to make the vision more concrete by helping people see how it will ultimately move the needle.

Cultural Competence

In an increasingly diverse and culturally complex world, executives need to lead people of all ages, races, sexual identities, religions, geographies, personal views, and abilities. What we see in our coaching practice is that today most leaders mean well, but they are often afraid of making mistakes that can offend people, and therefore they are holding back from having competent conversations where they can invite these aspects of diversity into the forefront, which we know ultimately drives performance. The data on this front is conclusive: McKinsey & Company's research found that companies in the top quartile for diversity are 35% more likely to have financial returns above their respective national industry medians.[6] A study by Boston Consulting Group (BCG) found that diverse teams generate 19% more revenue from innovation compared to non-diverse teams.[7] Even though companies have put a lot of effort in recent years in creating more diverse workplaces, our experience showed us that when it comes to creating a culture of inclusion and belonging, the missing link is the skill of "cultural competence."

Looking Forward

The coaching frameworks that we explore in this book will enable leaders to have capable and courageous conversations that can create an environment of true inclusion and belonging. Culturally competent leaders understand the multiple aspects of identity, and they regularly reflect on their own existing filters, beliefs, and habits. In this book, many of our frameworks will help you explore your out-of-comfort zones and unconscious biases, to help you become more culturally competent.

"The advice that sticks out the most is to have a coach. The one thing people are never good at is seeing themselves as others see them. A coach really, really helps."

—*Eric Schmidt, Former CEO of Google*

3

Fundamentals First: Leadership in Combination with Coaching

Leading with Coaching clearly has two fundamental components to it—that of leading and that of coaching.

The Fundamentals of Leading with Coaching

There are many views on what constitutes good leadership, so let's look at leadership through the lens of leadership in combination with coaching.

Defining Success

One of the most important aspects of Leading with Coaching is to establish what success looks like—where you are going, what you want to achieve, and your definition of collective success. In the past these answers often depended on what shareholders expected, yet today that is not enough. Yes, you need to set performance metrics, you need to know how to measure your progress against them, and you need to be able to demonstrate to stakeholders that you are being successful. However, today it is also just as important to wrap into your definition of success your purpose, your contribution to the world and to society, and to be clear on both how your moral and cultural compasses contribute to your success indicators.

People are less and less inclined to get out of bed simply to achieve a defined profit margin or level of market share. There needs to be more.

Involving Others

Leading with Coaching also means that you take the approach of wanting to co-build these metrics with your team rather than them being told what success looks like. This is a vital step as it addresses a fundamental human motivator—that of self-determination. If you have been involved in the crafting of the definition of what a good future looks like, you are so much more invested in the work needed to reach that. You own part of it; it is yours as you helped to define it. And that makes you so much more likely to accept and embrace the responsibility to deliver it. So, successful co-creation is an essential step of Leading with Coaching from the outset.

Staying Invested

Once you have a definition of success, Leading with Coaching means being invested in keeping teams and individuals engaged, focused, and enabled to deliver.

In today's world, distraction is everywhere. Complexity is distraction's best friend. Pressure and fear stalk organizations looking to derail, discombobulate, and sow discord. It is the combination of these specters that are most likely to move people away from their definition of success and toward many people's greatest fear—that of failure.

As a consequence, a great leader today has to have the intent and the ability to "absorb pressure, transmit clarity, and build the confidence in others that they need to succeed." Without confidence, a sense of optimism, and high levels of trust in our collective ability to problem-solve, it is close to impossible to thrive. It is the responsibility of any leader to create and maintain these conditions, regardless of the storm levels that may prevail around them.

Avoiding the Common Pitfalls

There are a number of mistakes we frequently see leaders make that need to be avoided. The first is the constant reinvention of the wheel or consistently changing the definition of success and reinventing the strategies needed to get there. That is not to say that if something isn't working it shouldn't be changed. Rather it is about getting the "what" right in the first place and then sticking to it long enough to prove that it will work, or if not, that it needs to be changed and a new success definition or strategy crafted.

A second frequent mistake is that leaders communicate something once, or maybe twice, and assume that a single message is enough to inculcate that message to a team, group, or entire organization. This is simply never true. Leaders need to repeat messages over and over again before they fully live. Focus on repeating the chorus; you can never do it too much.

Many leaders also make the mistake of praising the outcome of activity rather than the way the outcome was achieved. If a leader says in a group of people "Well done to Jo for hitting the sales target of US$10 million," the audience has learned nothing other than that Jo has been able to achieve something that perhaps they are struggling to do. If, on the other hand, a leader says "Jo, I would like to congratulate you on hitting the US$10 million sales target. I was particularly impressed at how you worked with the supply chain team to meet the client expectation. I thought your client relationship management really enabled a win-win to be negotiated with understanding on both sides of the need to compromise and help each other to meet both sides' goals and constraining factors. And I thought you did a great job liaising with and explaining to the finance team how they could help create a structure for the client and for us to be successful together. Well done." Now the audience knows not just the outcome that Jo achieved but more importantly they have learned *how* Jo achieved the outcome so that they can mimic or adapt her approach to help themselves succeed.

Of course, this takes more time than a simple "good job, well done" approach. And this is another mistake that leaders often make—not creating the time to do their leadership job. The job of a leader is to lead. Make sure that you structure your time accordingly.

Finally, be clear on the difference between being a manager and being a leader. A manager gets things done by other people. A leader helps others to understand how to make the best choices and decisions to achieve success.

> *"Leadership is not about being the best. Leadership is about making everyone else better."*
>
> —Simon Sinek

Case Study: Be a Bold Leader of Internal Brand

Very often, definitions of collective success can be thought of as internal brands. For example, we worked with a leadership team tasked with a major turnaround of their business in the food manufacturing sector. At the time the team started on the turnaround road, there was very little to celebrate. They were losing market share, their factories were inefficient, and productivity was poor. Their distribution was chaotic and unpredictable. Their people had little to no faith that the company could recover and were largely disengaged. Nobody seemed to have a recovery plan.

The leadership team came together to create a vision and a definition of collective success that needed to be compelling and so simple that it would be understood by the 1,000 members of the company despite the deep complexity of the challenge. After two days of wrestling with this, the team developed a single page that encapsulated the definition of success. At the heart of this was the slogan "10/10." This stood for the ambition to achieve a 10% increase in productivity and efficiency in the factories each year in order to drive 10% increase in net sales growth each year and to achieve a post-tax profitability target of 10% each year on gross sales. But it also stood for people giving 10/10 of their effort and achieving 10/10 of their potential as professionals in order to grow as people as well as to grow the business. It meant that each year, 10% more of their customers would access good quality food thereby improving the health of people and giving real societal purpose to the effort that this would require from all the employees.

(continued)

(continued)

Embedded into this was the clear expectation of the four behaviors that would be required to achieve the 10/10 ambition and three enablers that would help people to get there. This was then launched as an internal brand using posters on the walls of all the factories and offices, stickers on the trucks that distributed the product, and repeated in huddles and scrums. A theme song that was a beloved pop song was used to animate 10/10 along with videos, podcasts, e-mail signatures, and a host of other channels that kept the message live and top of mind. They encouraged their functional leadership teams to create their own plans as to how to contribute to 10/10 at a functional level so that there was an alignment cascade throughout the business to support the overall ambition. The leadership chorus was sung, effectively, into being.

This team was truly bold in the way they led this change. But they were also deceptively simple in tackling something deeply complex. As the company turned around and started to reach its goals, they celebrated successes focusing on how each success had been achieved. They developed the brand year on year moving from 10/10 to 10/10 *PLUS* as they started to exceed their initial targets. Three years into this exercise, they were growing at 25% per year. Quite a leadership achievement.

At the heart of this transformation was the implementation of a coaching approach to enable and empower people.

So, you can see that the Leading with Coaching approach has a requirement for thoughtful, consistent, and conscious leadership, which is then coupled with the core principles and skills of coaching.

The Anatomy of a Good Leader

The definition of what makes a good leader can be subjective, but ultimately, at the heart of good leadership is the ability to create a connection that will be powerful enough for people to follow you because they want to (influence), not because they have to (authority).

Think of your own experience with the leaders you have encountered in your career: what were the traits that made them most effective? How did they show up, what made them uniquely capable to create success?

There are different definitions of what makes for good leadership, but over our 20 years of working with top leaders and organizations around the world, we have seen five characteristics that the best leaders have in common, discussed next.

Ability to Influence Others

Data shows that influence is more powerful than authority when it comes to leadership. A *Harvard Business Review* report[1] showed that teams led by influential leaders outperform those led by authoritative or directive figures. Influential leadership styles contribute to a 15% higher profitability and a 21% increase in productivity, driven by employee motivation and alignment with organizational goals. In addition, influential leaders also boost innovation and creativity: a study by McKinsey[2] found that organizations with leaders who influence through inspiration and motivation, rather than authority, have a 70% higher chance of fostering innovative environments. These leaders encourage risk-taking and creative problem-solving, leading to greater organizational success.

Integrity

Leaders with a clear moral compass are the difference between going in the right direction, and getting lost or pointing in a direction that is not sustainable or right for an organization. Integrity is core to fostering trust and ethical behavior within the organization, and it helps make honest and transparent decisions that benefit the organization and its members. Data shows that integrity is crucial for long-term success and employee loyalty: research by the Edelman Trust Barometer[3] indicates that 67% of employees globally expect their leaders to exhibit integrity. High levels of trust in leadership, which is fostered by integrity, result in a 13% increase in employee engagement, and a 20% rise in job satisfaction. A study by the Ethics Resource Center[4] found that organizations with strong ethical cultures, led by leaders who prioritize integrity, experience a 16% higher return on assets and a 24% higher return on equity.

Empathy

Empathy is at the heart of creating the bonds that will make people choose to follow a leader, helping them connect with their team members on a personal level, understanding their needs, emotions, and perspectives. Empathetic leaders build strong relationships, enhance team cohesion, and create a supportive and inclusive work environment. Empathy is often an underrated driver of performance, as it sounds like a "soft skill," but data shows that it has a direct correlation in driving superior results: the "Global Empathy Index"[5] by the *Harvard Business Review* reveals that the top 10 companies in the empathy index generated 50% more earnings than the bottom 10 companies. These above-the-norm business results are often driven by empathetic leaders that create extraordinary employee engagement and retention:

research by Catalyst[6] found that companies with empathetic leaders are more likely to have highly engaged employees, are 87% less likely to leave their organizations, and 21% more productive than their less engaged counterparts.

Communication Skills

Great leaders are excellent communicators, both verbally and non-verbally. They convey clear expectations, listen actively, and ensure their team understands their roles and responsibilities. These skills are even more important in a world where organizations are global, people operate remotely, and there are countless layers of hierarchies, functions, and roles that get in the way of proximity. In the next few chapters, we go much deeper into some key communication skills, and explain how you can coach fellow leaders to become inspiring communicators who master the art of clarity. Additionally, one of the most underrated communication skills is not about speaking—it's active listening, which is key to emotionally intelligent leaders. We dive into that as well. Ultimately, leaders who communicate with emotional intelligence can build strong relationships with their teams. McKinsey reports that organizations where leaders communicate and coach effectively are nearly four times more likely to outperform their competitors.[7]

Resilience

Leaders who are resilient can adapt to challenges and bounce back from setbacks fast; they maintain a positive outlook, support their team through difficulties, and promote a culture of perseverance and continuous improvement. Now more than ever, in a Volatile, Uncertain, Complex, Ambiguous (VUCA) world, resilience is essential to navigating a dynamic and unpredictable business landscape. Resilient leaders drive organizational agility, which is crucial for maintaining performance in dynamic environments. McKinsey's findings suggest that leaders who foster resilience and adaptability within their teams contribute to a more agile and responsive organization.[8] This agility helps organizations navigate market changes and maintain a competitive edge. Recent research from IMD,[9] one of the most prestigious business schools globally, has shown that leaders who are able to bounce back from setbacks and manage stress effectively not only maintain their own performance but also support their teams in navigating pressure and uncertainty.

Looking Forward

In the next chapters of this book, we unpack some coaching techniques and frameworks that will help you coach fellow leaders to become more influential, define the values that are key to their integrity, expand their ability to create empathy, sharpen their communication skills, and build regular resilience practices.

"Leadership is hard to define, and good leadership even harder. But if you can get people to follow you to the ends of the earth, you are a great leader."

—*Indra Nooyi, Former CEO of PepsiCo*

CHAPTER

4

What People Want from Work

Another important aspect of Leading with Coaching is to fully understand as a leader what people want from work and therefore from you and the environment that you promote. The old days of assuming people want a job for life, leading to a pension and retirement, are irrelevant and impossible to deliver in today's world. Now, many people expect their emotional needs to be partly met by their colleagues and their work environment. They also expect their social values and purpose to be represented where they work. Many people want to know that what they do and how they do it in conjunction with others has a positive impact on the world, or at least that their organization has the conscience to mitigate any unavoidable harm derived from its activity.

Purpose and Authenticity

Purpose through work has become ever more important to attract and retain talent. It also drives engagement and discretionary effort. Leaders need to be able to honestly articulate the purpose of what an organization does in such a way as to be meaningful to the people who work in the organization and those who they serve. Of course, much of this is connected to the idea of storytelling and internal branding that you have already read about, but it requires more reference when leading individuals and teams. The constant referencing to the purpose, the importance of the way people think and work together, and the behaviors that leaders both authentically demonstrate and reward and praise are the essence of the culture that they create. No surprise then that the old adage that leading through example remains relevant and is, in fact, even more important if you choose to Lead with Coaching. When leaders say that they lead in a certain way but that is then not experienced by others, there is a very rapid, and often irreversible, reduction in belief and trust in that leader. Make sure you do as you say.

Case Study: Leading with Authenticity

A very senior leader we recently worked with in a fast-moving consumer business is a very credible commercial expert in her field. She genuinely cares for the people she leads and she wants to help them succeed. She talks often to her teams about how she views herself as a "servant leader" and in that role her intention is to coach people and teams to be the best they can be and thereby reach their extremely challenging target commercial outcomes. All very commendable and noble, you might think. The challenge she had was that people did not experience any of that. She was always late to meetings, constantly interrupted people, exercised a command-and-control style, and made it very clear that she was disappointed when people suggested that things get done in a different way than the way she had in mind.

In essence, she wanted intellectually to be the leader she talked of herself as being. Yet she lacked the emotional awareness to understand that she wasn't showing up like that at all. When people experience *cognitive dissonance*—when their experience is significantly different than their expectation of it—they rapidly lose trust and even move into a form of organ rejection. Our client was lucky enough to have a very good HR business partner who spotted what was going on before our leader was fully rejected. This partner hired an external Executive Coach. We did an extensive exercise of listening to how people were experiencing her leadership, which we were then able to feed back as accurate data to her. She was devastated when she understood what was happening, and she was rapidly able to address her behaviors and to apologize while giving people full permission to challenge her when she was not living up to her leadership promise. The moral of the story is that as someone who has chosen to Lead with Coaching, you have to live up to the promise and to demonstrate it while having the awareness to see yourself through the eyes of others.

Remuneration

Notwithstanding the need to authentically be what you claim to be, there are also many other aspects of leadership that are often underused. These mostly pertain to addressing the less tangible things that people want from work. Depending on the type of organization you work in, some of the weightings of these might change. For example, remuneration might have a higher weighting for people working in a bank than for those working in a green energy company. Money is important in both; it is just that it is more important to the people in one than the other. Many leaders have fallen into the trap that money is the most important and effective tool to deliver what people want from work. It might surprise you to know that our supposition is that, in most work environments, it represents only 20% of the levers available to leaders. This might rise to a maximum of 40% in certain defined environments, but in either case, it represents a minority of what a leader can focus on when engaging people in work.

What people actually want is comprised of a pizza pie of small pieces. The biggest single piece is money—we all have to earn a living. Yet all the other little slices that represent 5–10% each of the leadership pizza combine to be more powerful collectively than money.

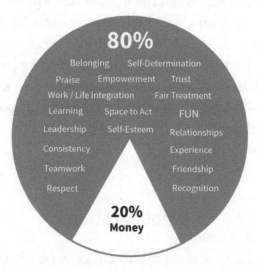

FIGURE 4.1 Studies Indicate That Money Is a Small Part of the Pie That Drives Satisfaction at Work

A Sense of Belonging

Most of these components of the pizza are intuitively what we all want. They address post-modern human nature, including that of purpose. It is not surprising that we all want a sense of safe community derived from working with others. Most of us want to learn, to develop, and to grow, personally and professionally. Many of us want respect for who we are and what we do, we want praise and recognition when we do something well, we want autonomy to decide and to influence. Teamwork, belonging, good relationships, fairness, and fun are all fairly basic human wants. Clear expectations and consistency help us perform and many of us derive pride from our performance. A frequently underused aspect is that work can be and should be fun. That does not mean drinking beer together or constantly playing soccer. It means that the way that we work, think, and achieve together is fun.

Flexibility

Another relatively new expectation in respect of what people want from work is flexibility. Post pandemic, people know that working flexibly is effective and liberating and can be effectively combined with being physically present with others. Our supposition is that flexibility is here to stay and that leaders need to embrace that.

Figure 4.1 shows how these leadership expectations can look.

You might think that this is completely obvious—and you would be right. The issue is how many leaders know all this and yet do not use any of it. Much of Leading with Coaching is raising from our unconscious mind to our conscious mind what we know to be true so that we can put it into practice—consciously, daily, and with purpose.

Taking Inventory of Your Leadership Levers

Sometimes, we find using some of these leadership levers difficult. For example, if you grew up in a household where praise was seen as inappropriate, rarely, if ever, used or even thought of as embarrassing, you are likely to underuse praise as a leadership lever. This can be corrected when you move it from your unconscious to your conscious. It moves from "something I never do" to "something I can do and want to do more of."

When you decide to Lead with Coaching, you are able to transcend your own default behaviors and become far more adept and aware of what you can do to help unlock someone else and their best thinking to achieve outstanding results. The reverse may also be true, so if you grew up in a household where praise was overused, you are likely to overuse it yourself as a leader. The result is that it is dismissed, as it seems disingenuous, therefore diminishing the impact of using it when it really counts.

It is worth thinking about doing an inventory of your leadership levers. What do you use well and appropriately; what do you overuse and could dial down; and what do you underuse that could help the people you lead become better and happier. After all, happy people are generally better workers.

"People want to feel that they matter and that their work is meaningful. They want to feel valued and recognized for their contributions."

—*Sheryl Sandberg, Former Facebook/Meta COO*

5

Coaching Fundamentals

There are two fundamental skills to the coaching part of Leading with Coaching—listening and questioning. These are the golden keys needed to unlock and unblock solutioning. They then need to be accompanied by critical convictions or beliefs about how we show up and conduct ourselves in our role as coach and what beliefs are needed about coaching to draw out all of its power.

Listening

Many of us think we know how to listen; after all, we have been listening to others all our lives. Or have we?

The ability to listen deeply is not innate. There is too much noise going on in our own heads. Thoughts get sparked by something someone says and distract us from the meaning and importance of what is being articulated, or we get emotionally triggered unconsciously part way through someone saying something. We listen impatiently to have our turn to speak, to reply, to give our side of the story or our point of view. We interrupt because we cannot contain ourselves. None of this is really *listening*.

> *"Courage is what it takes to stand up and speak. Courage is also what it takes to sit down and listen."*
>
> —*Winston Churchill*

The truth is that real listening comes about through deep concentration. It requires us to empty our minds and focus on another person and what they are saying. It means that we do not interrupt the person speaking and that we listen with our hearts, minds, eyes, and soul as much as we do with our ears. We are centered and highly curious when we are really listening. It's the same when we are deeply engaged with learning because learning and listening are very similar. We know when we are doing either well and most of the time we are not until we practice with conscious discipline.

Critically, when we are actively listening we are CALM—in Curious. Active. Listening. Mode.

Once we are listening in this fully engaged way, we can seek clarification using the technique of playback, where we say what we think we heard someone say to reassure them that we have really been listening and for them to expand on what we might not have captured, to seek clarification of meaning, and the technique of splitting to allow for the existence of contradiction. Figure 5.1 shows a few examples and techniques to help you show the other person clear signals that you are actively listening in a CALM way.

Playback
"OK, so let me try and capture what I think you said . . ."
Playback and allow the person to build on your playback

Work hard not to interrupt
"I notice your energy levels really increased when you were speaking about . . ."
Observe body language signals and energy levels.

Meaning
"It would help me to understand better what you mean by 'disappointed' . . ."
Allow the person to clarify.

Splitting
"Would it be right to think that a part of you feels X . . . and maybe another part is also a bit Y?"
Splitting to help people think about things they might naturally defend or reject.

FIGURE 5.1 The CALM Listening Model

Questioning

From an early age, we are encouraged with the statement that there is no such thing as a stupid question. This is true but that is not the same as defining which questions are great questions that move someone's thinking forward, that unlock and unblock. Later, this chapter looks at some specific structures that are particularly powerful to use as a coach. For the time being, let's stick to a reminder of the basic premises of good coaching questions.

Asking Good Questions

Behind good questions is the supposition that the person we are coaching has the capacity to find solutions when asked the right questions and are then listened to carefully. This is a critical mindset for anyone in the role of coach. Most of us have evidence that this supposition is the reality. Think of a time when you have been mulling something over, perhaps time and again, in your mind and not making progress toward a solution or clarity on the subject. Then, someone asks you to explain out loud what you are grappling with and really listens to you. As you speak, you become clearer, the articulation helps you to find a range of possible solutions or actions that could help drive a solution. This is not a rare occurrence for many of us when someone is generous enough to approach us with the will to curiously listen—what is rare is that, sadly, people do not do that very often for each other. As a coach, this is one of our superpowers so we will do it as often as possible.

There is a significant difference between someone questioning with the intent to unlock and unblock our thinking versus to manipulate us to think as they do, to surreptitiously impose their answer on us or simply to tell us what they think we should do. We feel the difference quickly and acutely and often resent it when we feel someone's intent is to control us, our thinking, or our choices. The secret to great questions as a coach lies in the purity of our intent and our questions.

Primarily, we will use open questions in which there is no suggestion of the solution or the *right*, in our opinion, way to think about something. This allows for creativity to evolve, it allows us to explore, it keeps us open to possibility. It lowers the frustration we can feel when we sense that something is being imposed on us that doesn't actually belong to us.

Open questions include:
- Tell me more about the issue?
- As you speak, are you becoming any clearer on what might help you?
- What does your gut tell you?
- What do you think is the truth about this issue?
- What would you think of doing if you were not afraid or had no constraints?

Closed questions include:
- It sounds to me that you should . . .

- Can't you see that . . . .
- I think you should do . . .
- I've been through this and let me tell you . . . .

We all know these concepts but that doesn't mean that we all apply our knowledge frequently enough to actually help people think things through for themselves and therefore fully own what they need to do next.

Suggestive Questioning

Sometimes, as a leader, it is helpful to share our experience and wisdom and this is especially so when someone asks us directly what we think their approach to an issue should be. However, even in these circumstances we should, as coaches, approach with caution by using suggestive questioning rather than directive statements. Suggestive questions might include ones such as "What do you think would happen if you did. . . . .?," or "When I went through something similar, I approached it this way, do you think that could help you in your current circumstances?" In other words, we are giving the person the freedom to accept or reject the suggestion by making it a choice, itself a question.

Forward Momentum: How Coaching Can Take You from Reflection to Action

Clients and people curious about coaching often ask us what the difference is between coaching and other disciplines like consulting, therapy, or even mentoring.

Many disciplines focus on the past or the present, but the fundamental focus of coaching is in helping create forward momentum, through a process in which a client and a coach partner in building their capability to achieve short- and long-term professional and personal goals.

Forward momentum is essential to coaching, for three reasons:

- **It builds motivation:** Seeing progress and experiencing forward momentum can boost motivation and confidence. It reinforces the client's belief in their ability to succeed and encourages them to continue their efforts.

- **It helps overcome resistance:** Forward momentum helps clients overcome resistance and inertia that may arise when pursuing challenging goals. By maintaining momentum, clients are less likely to get stuck or give in to obstacles and setbacks.

- **Develops adaptability:** Forward momentum in coaching is not just about linear progress but also about adaptability. Coaches help clients adjust their approach as needed, pivot when circumstances change, and maintain momentum even in the face of challenges.

Check Your Biases at the Door

When we are in coaching mode, a key skill to be able to genuinely help our clients is to be able to suspend judgment, stay open minded, and be able to look at the world through the lens of our client, not through our own.

We might not realize this, but our worldview and values inform a lot of our unconscious biases, which in turn become a filter for how we see and judge others. For example, if one of your core values is fairness, and in a coaching conversation you are confronted with a client that in your view is not being fair, you are likely to form a negative opinion of that, and this bias can trickle in your coaching demeanor, even in subtle ways: from the tone of your questions to your ability to stay neutral, will probably be impacted by this, creating an invisible yet palpable tension in the relationship.

When coaches go through training and certification, we are taught to suspend judgment as it plays a number of key roles in a coaching relationship:

- **Building trust and safety** by establishing a non-judgmental environment. When coaches suspend judgment, they create a safe space where clients feel free to express themselves without fear of criticism or bias. This trust is fundamental for a productive coaching relationship.

- **Openness.** Clients are more likely to open up about their true thoughts, feelings, and challenges when they know they won't be judged. Shame is an immediate reaction to judgment, and when clients sense that they will be judged, they will not dare to be vulnerable.

- **Uncovering true issues.** Clients are more likely to explore and discuss underlying issues when they feel accepted and understood, and they are likely to go into a zone where they can confide in the coach, which ultimately will benefit the depth of the process.

- **Enhancing listening and understanding,** suspending judgment allows for a more active form of listening to understand the client's perspective without preconceived notions or biases. In turn, this helps create empathy and connection, as you can better understand and support the client's unique experiences and needs.

- **Creative thinking.** A judgment-free environment encourages clients to explore new ideas and approaches without fear of making mistakes or being judged. They will be more willing to take risks and try new things, which can lead to significant breakthroughs and growth.

Suspending judgment is a practice and a skill that will benefit you not only as a coach, but also as a leader.

Self-reflection is a powerful tool for coaches to examine their own judgments and biases and understand how these might affect their coaching practice. In order to create a practice of suspending judgment, here are some prompts that will help you build a regular habit of checking your biases at the door.

SELF-REFLECTION PROMPTS FOR COACHES

Identifying my judgments and biases:

- What are some immediate judgments or assumptions I notice when I first meet a new client?
- How do I feel about clients who have different values, beliefs, or lifestyles from my own?
- Are there certain topics or issues that trigger a strong emotional response in me? What are they and why?
- How do my judgments and biases align or conflict with my values as a coach?

Understanding the impact they have on my coaching practice:

- How might my judgments and biases influence the questions I ask and the way I listen?
- In what ways could my biases affect the feedback and support I offer to clients?
- Can I recall a specific instance where my judgment or bias may have impacted a coaching session? What happened and what was the outcome?
- In what ways can I hold myself accountable for minimizing bias and judgment in my coaching practice?

Deepening my client relationship:

- How do I build rapport with clients who are very different from me? What challenges do I face in these situations?
- How do I ensure I create a safe and non-judgmental space for all my clients?
- What strategies do I use to remain open and curious about my clients' perspectives and experiences?

Creating opportunities for self-awareness and growth:

- How do I become aware of my judgments and biases in the moment? What signs do I look for in my body, my mind, my energy, and demeanor?
- What steps do I take to address and manage my biases when they arise?
- How do I seek feedback from clients and peers to understand how my biases may be perceived?

Developing mindfulness and presence:

- How do I practice mindfulness and presence to stay fully engaged and non-judgmental during coaching sessions?
- What techniques or practices help me to center myself and clear my mind before a coaching session, to make sure that I stay in a judgment-free zone?
- How do I recover and refocus when I notice my mind wandering or judgments creeping in during a session?

(continued)

(continued)

Commitment to continuous learning:

- What resources (books, articles, training) am I using to educate myself about unconscious bias and its effects?
- How do I incorporate learning about diversity, equity, and inclusion into my professional development?
- What goals can I set for myself to improve my ability to suspend judgment and manage biases in my coaching practice?

By regularly reflecting on these prompts, you can develop greater self-awareness and take proactive steps to minimize the impact of your judgments and biases on your coaching practice.

In conclusion, suspending judgment is fundamental to effective coaching. It enhances trust, promotes client autonomy, fosters authentic self-expression, and encourages innovative thinking. By cultivating a non-judgmental stance, coaches can provide a supportive and empowering environment that facilitates profound client growth and development.

Beware of Projection

In coaching, projection refers to the psychological phenomenon where the client or even the coach unconsciously attributes their own feelings, thoughts, or traits onto another person. This can occur when people are unaware of certain aspects of themselves and, instead of recognizing these qualities within, they see them in others.

While projection can offer valuable insights into the client's inner world, it poses risks in a coaching context. If unaddressed, it can distort the client's perception of their challenges and relationships, hinder self-awareness, and potentially strain the coach-client relationship by creating misunderstandings or misplaced expectations. Coaches must be attuned to signs of projection to guide the client toward greater self-understanding and to maintain a clear, objective coaching process.

Some real-life signs of projection will come up in everyday language of your coachee, and these are some common themes that you might encounter:

- **Blaming others:** "Everyone at work is so negative; they just don't understand how hard I work." "My boss is always stressed out, and it makes my job impossible."

- **Overgeneralizations:** "No one ever listens to my ideas; they just don't care about what I have to say." "People always take advantage of my kindness."

- **Unexplained strong reactions:** "I can't stand how arrogant that person is!" (When there's no clear evidence of arrogance.) "That person is so lazy, it drives me crazy." (When the behavior may not align with the intensity of the reaction.)

- **Projecting personal feelings:** "They're clearly jealous of me because I'm more successful." "She's always angry with me for no reason" (When the client may actually be harboring anger themselves).

- **Transferring personal fears or insecurities:** "I think they're avoiding me because they know I'm not good enough." "They don't trust me, even though I've given them no reason to doubt."

When you hear phrases like these, it's important to explore further to determine whether the client is projecting their own feelings or experiences onto others. Gently asking questions like, "What makes you feel that way?" or "Is it possible that this might be more about how you're feeling?" can help bring projection to the surface for examination.

Projective identification is also a defense mechanism in which the individual projects qualities that are unacceptable to their "Self" onto another person. The Self rejects inner parts that are undesirable and "sub-contracts" or projects onto someone else to fill those gaps.

It happens in all of us, and it is a rich source for exploration in Executive Coaching. As a leader-coach we need to be aware of our own inner dynamics to prevent transference of projective identification to our client as well. If you notice signs of projection, gently bring them to the client's attention. Discuss how their thoughts or feelings might be influenced by their own experiences rather than by others.

Case Study: Projection in Coaching: The Man with One Black Shoe

By Nathalie van der Poel, Executive Coach

Let me share with you the story of the man with the one black shoe.

Years ago I worked with a client, let's call him William. He had a very successful career so far, having become the director of a big R&D facility for a technical multinational. William told me he despised his bosses and found it very difficult to respect them and adhere to their decisions. This happened with each new manager he got and had become a limiting factor in his career.

When we explored underlying dynamics, William said he always started off with working very hard for any new boss.

He would go out of his way to prove himself, reach the desired objectives and even predict what his manager would like and would be positively surprised by, to impress him. This would earn him excellent appraisals and rapid promotions. However, usually after a period of a year or so, William would become cynical, depreciative of his manager, and would start to complain about the many shortcomings his manager had.

When we dissected this mechanism, William discovered he worked so hard for each of his managers to feel "good enough" and to earn love, appreciation, and a sense of belonging, only to find out none of his managers would give him what he needed to the extent he craved. When asked what this deep desire was about, William told me his father had left the family when he was five, and that he had never heard from his father since. He resonated deeply with the fact that he never received recognition, love, or pride from his father and subconsciously projected these deep longings onto other men in his life with authority over him.

The realization that these people could never match the expectations he had from them and would never be able to heal the deep scars of growing up without a father, was the start of William's transformation.

When asked at the end of this particular session what he would do now as a first step, William answered: "I will go and get a new pair of black brogue shoes." This surprised me and I nearly fell into my own pitfall of asking: "Why?"

William continued by saying: "When my father left, my mother got rid of everything that reminded her of him. My siblings and I grew up in a house without a trace of our father. The only thing that I discovered in the back of

(continued)

(continued)

the cupboard after he left, was this one black brogue shoe. I cherished and held on to it for many years.

Now that I am aware of how I projected all my frustrations and desires related to my father, onto my subsequent managers, I need to accept that they will never be able to make me feel 'whole' again and that I need to do that myself. I will buy a new pair of exactly the same black brogue shoes and each time I wear them, it will remind me that I cannot make others responsible for what I missed in my life."

When I met William again a month or so later, he seemed a different man. He seemed softer, more open, and more inquisitive. He wore his black brogue shoes. We were silent for a long time and then he said: "for a week or so, every time I put on my shoes I cried, then for a week or so I was furious, and since a week or so I wear my shoes with pride. It is as if I have a part of my father with me every day. The good part."

This story taught me a couple of important lessons as a coach:

- We should never underestimate how incredibly powerful projective identification can be in determining relationships with important stakeholders.

- We should also never underestimate the resourcefulness of the client . . . He bought new shoes, and who am I to judge that. Perhaps against my first belief, this solution worked marvelously for him.

- As coaches, we need to be very aware of our own projective identification mechanisms and transference traps. There is a part in me, that wishes to be acknowledged for my "brilliant coaching." With William, he found his own brilliant and creative way of moving forward. It left me humbled, touched, and incredibly proud of him.

Adopting a Coaching Mindset

Leading with Coaching also requires you to have the right attitude and mindset as well as the belief that coaching really works.

Some of this is in opposition to how you might have been raised to believe that the world works or what it values. For example, knowledge, being an expert, has been either a tacit or explicit expectation of leaders. We believe that we are expected to have the answers. Yet as coaches, we need to get really comfortable with the idea of going with the not knowing.

NOTE: Your value does not lie in the provision of answers but rather in the facilitation of others to find solutions that really work. With the advent of AI, knowledge is a commodity with a declining value. The value of a leader of the future lies not in their subject expertise but in their ability to take others through change and uncertainty.

You also need to accept and understand that the time you spend coaching someone is often only the catalyst of their thinking; you do not need to walk away with the solutions or answers clear and agreed and wrapped up with a bow.

A coaching relationship requires a foundation of deep trust. This includes the fact that in a one-to-one setting what is said remains entirely confidential and will not get fed back in settings that might not maintain confidentiality and trust. It is also critical that the content of a coaching session is never used against the person being coached by means of satiating ego or worse, in a form of bullying. Coaching by nature requires an environment of psychological safety. Particularly because, if we are in any way afraid, we run the risk that our flight or fight response is triggered by the release of adrenalin and cortisol, the hormone most associated with stress. When either of those are released, they close down our prefrontal cortex, which is the part of our brain primarily responsible for us to find solutions.

Leading Through Coaching takes practice, especially of the fundamentals. Once you have mastered these, you can move on to grow your skills.

"One of the most important aspects of leadership is to have a growth mindset. Coaching plays a crucial role in fostering this mindset by helping leaders to continuously learn and evolve."

—*Satya Nadella, CEO of Microsoft*

6

The Magic of Storytelling: Emotional Leadership

Much of Leading with Coaching, especially with teams or groups of people, lies in the leader's ability to engage those in organizations in what needs to be done and the reasons this is important. Communicating a collective definition of success is powerful and can then be used as a cascade for what different teams and even individuals need to contribute to success. This helps act as a compass for everyone to remain on track to not only do what is needed but also think about how they do that. It is about exercising the art and magic of storytelling.

It has always been surprising to us how little importance many leaders put on the need to communicate and engage. There tends to be little thought as to how best to communicate, what communication structures work best, and how to appeal to an audiences' brains and hearts in equal measure. That said, some leaders do this incredibly well and seemingly with little effort. So, we did a seven-year study to see if there were commonalities between the way great leaders communicate with great effect and how average leaders communicate with average effect. The results were clear and perhaps not surprising when deconstructed.

I think most people have suffered the pain and boredom of the 30, 40, or more slide PowerPoint presentation. These typically start with a predictable structure:

- Let me tell you about me and what makes me credible (5 slides).

- Let me tell you about my expertise and how clever I am on this topic (10 slides).

- Let me give you all the context I know about this topic and what makes it important to us (15 slides).

- Let me give you the plan and project management scheme for what we will do (10 slides).

- Let me tell you the advantages to our organization of (me) doing this work (10 slides).

- Finally, let me explain what success this will bring to our organization (1 slide).

At what point did you start smiling while reading that and thinking of a time when you had to sit through exactly that presentation? With all of the 51 slides flashing before your eyes? Perhaps you remembered all the senior people in the room interrupting with questions and ideas because they had no idea where the presenter was taking the room?

Yet it is unfair to blame the presenter—this is how most of us are taught to build presentations, and we simply do our best to deliver against expectations of the norm. Unfortunately, this average approach leads to average impact.

Tricks from the Best

What do great leaders do differently to great effect? To skip to the end of the findings of our extensive study, what we learned was that great leaders never use a conventional communication structure or presentation structure. If there is any similarity at all, it is that they start at the end by first of all laying out clearly and simply what success looks like in terms of the subject they are about to address. This helps keep the audience focused on the end goal and makes the rest of the content and flow logical and relevant as to how it supports the success statement given up front.

They also understand that they need to focus on the attitude or the behaviors needed to achieve success and to be explicit about these. They know that the way we think and work together is one of the most important factors to drive successful outcomes.

Only then do they talk about the relevant context such as the competitive environment or the case for change.

They further understand that nobody champions change unless they fully understand firstly the benefit of that change to them personally and secondly the benefit of that change to the community or team that they belong to.

The final piece of the puzzle they understand is what gets measured gets made, so they describe how they will measure success.

The Emotional Leadership Flow

By adopting this structure, it is easy for the audience to grasp what is being suggested from a logical point of view—it makes sense—and also from an emotional point of view because it is accessible from a personally motivating perspective. It has an emotional impact on the audience as well as making sense.

This is the reason that we coined this communication structure the Emotional Leadership Flow, as shown in Figure 6.1.

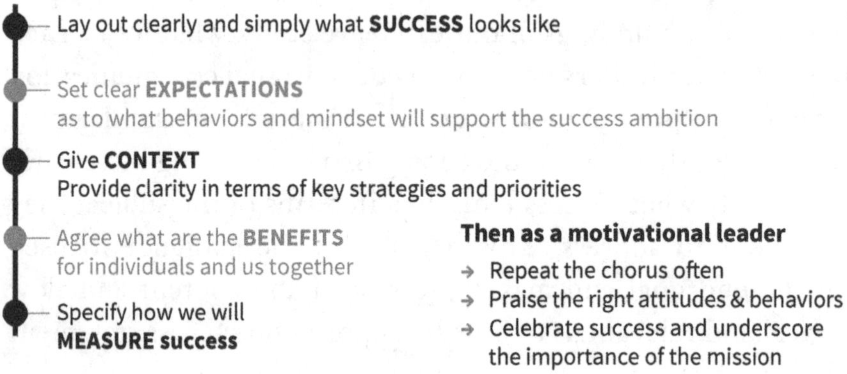

- Lay out clearly and simply what **SUCCESS** looks like

- Set clear **EXPECTATIONS**
  as to what behaviors and mindset will support the success ambition

- Give **CONTEXT**
  Provide clarity in terms of key strategies and priorities

- Agree what are the **BENEFITS**
  for individuals and us together

- Specify how we will
  MEASURE success

Then as a motivational leader

→ Repeat the chorus often
→ Praise the right attitudes & behaviors
→ Celebrate success and underscore
  the importance of the mission

FIGURE 6.1 The Emotional Leadership Flow

We could cite many leaders who have given memorable speeches that have, in some cases, quite literally changed the world using this structure. Some for the better and some for the worse. It is worthy of note that those intent on evil are often better at using this process than those intent on doing good. However, to give examples of those leaders who were motivated to do good and who have used this structure often, we would include Nelson Mandela, Barack Obama, and Winston Churchill, among many others.

Of course, this structure is not only used on global or nation-wide stages. Mostly it is now used by great communicators and leaders taking people on a journey, usually of change, involving them in the story, fueling their imagination as to what success can look like and how they can play a part in that. This can be done for an entire organization, it can be done for a function, and it can be done for a group of people who need to collaborate or a team with specific responsibility. It can even be used all the way down to setting up an individual for success for the year or for a project. It is usually best for the leader to do a first draft of the flow and then to discuss (one could even use the word negotiate) the specific content of each section with the person or team to co-create the story. Once written, the flow can be used to track progress over the year or for one-to-one meetings with direct reports to see how they are developing over time. It allows for teams to track their delivery against their ambition and to improve as learnings occur. It is also a fantastic entry point into the coaching relationship between the person or team and their leader as it allows for visibility on what is working and what is not yet working at any point. The coaching conversations can then focus on amplifying and accelerating what is working and allow for exploration around what needs to change to make the things that are not yet working better. It also allows for the coaching conversation to be around any part of the Emotional Leadership Flow—it could be around the need to change the success definition, it might be a behavioral or attitudinal shift, it might be because the context has changed leading to other adjustments, or it might be about the motivation or benefit perception. Or it could be to address a performance gap identified by measurement. And as these coaching conversations unfold, the document itself can be evolved such that it lives.

NOTE: We purposely called this structure Emotional Leadership because, done well, it has the ability to connect the brain (logic) with the heart (emotion), and when those two connect the impact is far greater than when only one is engaged.

The art to using this highly engaging communication structure is practice, because while it looks simple to use, it takes a while to truly get the hang of what goes into each section.

The following sections describe some examples of how the completed flow can look.

Example 1: Setting a Team Up for Success

In this example, a team of lawyers work on a client transaction.

Success

Our client wishes to acquire the telecom assets of company X in the state of Montana.

These assets will enhance our client's ability to offer rapid fiber optic services to the entire state, thereby increasing its ability to grow market share and to speed up client acquisition rates.

This is now time sensitive as negotiations between the parties have been ongoing for several months, slowing down our client's growth plans in Montana. So we have 30 days in which to complete this transaction.

This will require us to work closely as a team, making clear who is responsible for what and by when for each component of the transaction and for each phase of the transaction.

Clear and timely communication between the team and regular updates to the client will be critical since the client is concerned about any slippage in the time it takes to complete the transaction.

We will be focused on pragmatic commercial solutions that serve our client's interests while also protecting our client's interests—our client expects us to act as facilitators of this acquisition finding creative solutions to any barriers that we come across. They do not expect us to be transaction police so focused on managing risk that we become blockers of getting the transaction done within the required time line.

This a major opportunity for our firm to deepen the relationship with this client who has traditionally used other firms for transactions of this size. This is a moment to create high trust between our firm and our client and to show them just what we are capable of achieving on their behalf—so this is an exciting opportunity for us as a team and as a firm.

Expectations

As a team delivering on the success requirement outlined previously, we need to adopt clear attitudes and behaviors; we must be **highly collaborative** and **communicate transparently**, we need to adopt a **solution-focused mindset**, be clear at all times on roles, responsibilities, and delivery timetables and we must demonstrate that we are lawyers with the ability to act in a **commercial and pragmatic** way to achieve our client's goals with them.

Context

This transaction is a strategic imperative to the firm as we pivot toward being a firm that is known for our understanding of telecoms infrastructure expertise and our ability to help clients upgrade their infrastructure such that it can be better leveraged to provide content that customers want at speeds they demand.

The market, both prospective clients in the sector and other law firms, will be watching this transaction carefully as a barometer of our ability to fulfill our promise to clients.

In the wings are other transactions that we could anticipate winning if we are seen as doing a good job on this mandate—notably in California and Texas.

Benefits

While this transaction is likely to require a lot of work from the team in the next 30 days, we will all have the ability to learn and to upskill while we advise on this transaction. Particularly, we will hone our client relationship management skills, as we will all interact with the client regularly during the process. So this is a tremendous learning opportunity both from a technical perspective and also from an interpersonal perspective.

For us as a team, it is an opportunity to build our reputation and earn the recognition and respect of the market. By focusing on our individual ability to contribute to our collective success, we will bond as a team and hopefully have some fun through the process.

Measuring Success

We will measure how we are doing as a team each week in terms of the deliverables and how we work together by giving and accepting live feedback. These team meetings will be held for an hour each Monday morning.

At the same time, we will actively seek feedback from the client and respond to that feedback as we receive it.

Finally, we will deliver the transaction in the 30-day time frame required by the client to their satisfaction. And we will celebrate our success together at the end of the transaction—something I personally look forward to.

Example 2: Delivering a Proposal to a Board or Articulating a Vision

This example discusses a financial institution with the ambition to establish a digital bank in Turkey.

Success

Within three years we will have established a new bank in Turkey that will be fully and solely digital, attracting a young demographic of clients that will produce additional group profits of US$1 billion per annum in phase one of its establishment.

Our focus on the young demographic will allow us to provide a unique suite of products and services designed for and around our clearly defined target client. It will also allow us to grow with our customers as they themselves grow their economic relevance and to service them throughout their banking lives.

Our setup costs will be considerably lower than those of the established competitors as we leap-frog directly to digital and avoid costly infrastructure investment. Further, our direct to digital approach will allow us to provide outstanding customer service through our digital platforms as well as through voice support. Our early adoption of artificial intelligence will give us a far higher level of predictability of customer behaviors and greater agility to adapt to changing customer wishes.

Expectations

In order to succeed with our vision, we will need to **learn fast**, we will need to **adapt in real time**, we will need to be **creative**, and we will need to **leave behind many of our more traditional approaches** to how we have done business to date with the legacy business we operate in many other markets.

Context

Here are some remarkable statistics about the demographics of the Turkish population:

- The median age is 34 years
- 48.3% of the population is under the age of 30
- 24.4% is between the ages of 15–29
- 75.1% of the population is urban

This makes it the most attractive market in Europe to start a digital only bank.

While the country has had some economic and geopolitical challenges, the long-term prospects for economic growth are fundamentally strong.

The competitive environment is largely populated by local banks with high-cost infrastructure and legacy technology that is difficult to modernize at speed. Yet the sector posted record profits in 2022, making it an extremely profitable sector.

Benefits

Through this investment, the board has the opportunity to show its ability to operate in a way that it has not proven yet in other markets. This will build the confidence of our stakeholders and shareholders.

For the wider organization, this enterprise will allow us to test and learn in a new market which will then allow us to adopt and scale in our traditional markets. This will drive organizational-wide performance, drive up return on capital, and open a new and profitable market with enormous growth potential, which is currently lacking.

Measuring Success

We will measure our success through reaching our target profitability in Turkey by the end of year three and by measuring how much best practice can be transferred effectively to drive profitability elsewhere in the group.

Looking Forward

These examples of the structure of Emotional Leadership are adapted from some of our work with clients, and offered by means of illustration only. However, they are designed to help you think how you could improve the magic of your own leadership storytelling, how you can improve how you set people up to succeed, and then how you support them through Leading with Coaching.

"Stories are just data with a soul. If you want to make a connection, you have to tell the story."

—*Brené Brown, Author, Researcher, and Speaker*

7

Beliefs and How They Influence Leadership Styles

Our beliefs play a massive role in everything we do, but most people don't take the time to examine them to understand how they impact us day to day. In essence, our beliefs are a core part of our operating system: we are not consciously aware of them, but they run the show in many surprising ways.

If you want to gain self-awareness as a leader, understanding and examining your beliefs is key: beliefs shape a leader's perspective, decision-making process, and overall approach to leading others.

Most people think of beliefs as intellectual thoughts or commitments to certain ideals ("I believe in a lean government," "I believe in God"), when in fact they are much more fundamental. A belief is the mental acceptance that something is true or exists, often without empirical evidence to prove it. Beliefs can be about various aspects of life, including opinions, values, or expectations about the future. Beliefs are the building blocks of our experience and how we see the world. In other words: the brain is made of neurons; the mind is made of beliefs.

The interesting thing about beliefs is that we create them, and therefore when we start examining them, we can also change them. You may have heard the expression "our beliefs create our reality," and this is indeed the case. Every belief we hold is like a tiny reality-creating machine of sensations, viewpoints about oneself or the world, limitations, or possibilities. Once created, our beliefs continue to do their job in helping us interpret the world, until we consciously challenge or shift them.

Looking at Core Beliefs

Research in the field of beliefs shows that on average, every person has tens of thousands of beliefs that operate in their lifetime. We also know that there are different levels of beliefs: the majority are what are called general or superficial beliefs, which typically operate at a conscious level. At a deeper level in our subconscious we have our core beliefs, which are fewer but much more powerful and deep-seated.

Unlike superficial beliefs, core beliefs are often formed very early in life, and they are closely related with our experience growing up within our family or in our immediate environment.

In our decades of experience coaching leaders across geographies, industries, and seniority levels, we have found that there are essentially three areas of core beliefs that have the greatest influence on how people show up as leaders in a work environment:

- Collaboration vs. competition
- Scarcity vs. abundance
- Safety vs. danger

Collaboration vs. Competition

These beliefs are created as a result of your early peer interactions, either within your family, or in your immediate environment at school. For example, families with multiple siblings typically nurture one or the other dynamic: in some cases, the parents reward collaboration in sibling relationships, whereas in other family units it can be easy to see that parents create distinctions and comparisons between kids, which ultimately feeds a subconscious belief that in order to get love and affection, you need to be better or different than your siblings. These dynamics are also experienced at an early age in our peer environments: at school, in playgroups, or sport environments. Kids are sponges, and they very quickly come to conclusions for what strategy is serving them best: collaborating or competing with peers, and they will adapt and adjust their behavior to favor that strategy.

These experiences over time become core beliefs that deeply influence how we show up in a professional context: leaders who believe in collaboration are naturally adept at being team players, and they lead teams in a way that creates a visible sense of collective cohesion and alignment toward shared goals. Leaders who have a core belief that prioritizes the value of competition are often calibrating themselves against their peers in order to "win" or be the best, and they lead teams with a style that tends to favor individual performance, drawing comparisons and creating a sense of competition among peers and with other teams.

SELF-REFLECTION PROMPTS:

- How do I typically operate: do I see myself tending toward collaboration or competition?

- Where does that come from?
- How is it helping me as a leader?
- How is it potentially getting in the way of my leadership goals?

Scarcity vs. Abundance

These beliefs are typically shaped by the culture, values, and reality of a family and later as an individual in society around access to money, opportunities, and resources. It is tempting to assume that people with a better financial environment will be more likely to have an abundance mindset, and people who experience hardships will tend to have a scarcity mindset, but reality shows that it is often more complex than that. For example, people may grow up in a family without financial hardships, but if their values prioritize frugality and restraint, they are more likely to operate in a scarcity mindset. Society and even religion can also play a major role in shaping these beliefs: in some social environments, lifestyle cues that signal wealth are encouraged and often admired, whereas in other contexts they are shunned or considered inappropriate displays.

It is important to note that abundance and scarcity mindsets are not necessarily binary categories: individuals may exhibit elements of both mindsets depending on the situation. Furthermore, people can experience both realities growing up, going from "good times" to "tough times," and they learn to adapt to the environment and operate effectively regardless of the context.

In terms of how scarcity and abundance beliefs can influence our style and behavior in a professional context, we have observed that leaders who operate from a mindset of abundance typically have a few common characteristics:

- They have a positive outlook, and they believe that there are plentiful opportunities, resources, and possibilities available to them. They tend to focus on what they have rather than what they lack.

- They are more likely to embrace growth, learning, and new experiences. They see challenges as opportunities for growth and improvement, rather than insurmountable obstacles.

- They lead with generosity and are naturally supportive and collaborative.

Leaders who have beliefs influenced by a mindset or a context of scarcity tend to:

- Focus on limitations, constraints, and potential losses. They often experience fear, anxiety, and worry about not having enough resources, opportunities, or time.

- Exhibit competitive behavior and a tendency to hoard resources. They may feel the need to constantly protect what they have and view others as potential threats.

- Lean toward a more fixed mindset, believing that their abilities, opportunities, and circumstances are limited and unlikely to change. This can lead to feelings of helplessness and resignation.

SELF-REFLECTION PROMPTS:

- How do I typically operate: do I tend to have a mindset of scarcity or abundance?
- Where does that come from?
- How do I show up when I lead from a mindset of abundance?
- How do I show up when I lead from a mindset of scarcity?
- How do they each serve me?
- How are they potentially getting in the way of my leadership goals?

Safety vs. Danger

These beliefs are typically more subtle and nuanced than the previous two areas, and they are often a combination of psychological, emotional, and environmental factors. These beliefs ultimately influence how leaders show up based on if they view the world as a fundamentally safe place, or a dangerous place.

The lived experiences that shape these core beliefs include:

- **Emotional safety:** The well-developed attachment theory from psychology posits that early interactions with caregivers play a foundational role in shaping beliefs about safety and danger. Kids who experience consistent, responsive, and nurturing caregiving are more likely to develop a sense of security and trust in their environment. On the other hand, inconsistent or neglectful caregiving can lead to feelings of insecurity and vigilance.

- **Day-to-day behaviors around risks and danger:** As kids, we learn about safety and danger by observing adults. If they demonstrate cautious and safety-conscious behavior, children are more likely to internalize similar beliefs, and exposure to risky situations without appropriate guidance can contribute to opposite beliefs of threat.

- **Traumatic experiences:** Events such as accidents, natural disasters, or violence can profoundly impact our beliefs about safety and danger. Depending on the nature and severity of the trauma, we develop hypervigilance, avoidance, or a sense of helplessness.

In our experience coaching individuals with both mindsets and beliefs, we have observed some common characteristics. Leaders that have a worldview where they believe that their environment is fundamentally safe typically:

- **Are very adept at building trust**, and they create a supportive environment where people feel psychologically safe to express their ideas, voice concerns, and take calculated risks.

- **Encourage collaboration**, teamwork, and open communication. They foster a sense of unity and support among team members, promoting cooperation and shared goals.

- **Invest in development** and recognize the importance of continuous learning. They value mentorship and opportunities for personal growth, empowering their teams to thrive and succeed.

People who experienced environments that shaped them to have dominant beliefs of danger can lead with a style in which they:

- **Emphasize risk management,** are attentive to threats, vulnerabilities, and challenges. They are cautious in decision-making and proactive in mitigating or avoiding risks.

- **Focus on accountability** and responsibility among team members. They set clear expectations and are explicit about the consequences of not meeting these expectations.

- **Monitor and control** processes, resources, and outcomes to ensure compliance and risk reduction.

Keep in mind that at the end of the day, effective leadership requires a balance between promoting safety and managing risks. The best leaders are capable of assessing situations in context, and they adapt their approach accordingly. For example, in times of uncertainty or crisis, leaders may need to prioritize safety measures and reassure their teams, while during periods of innovation and growth, they can encourage calculated risk-taking and experimentation. Ultimately, leaders who can navigate between beliefs of safety and danger effectively can create resilient, high-performing teams and organizational cultures that thrive in dynamic and challenging environments.

SELF-REFLECTION PROMPTS:

- What is my most dominant belief: do I see the world as a fundamentally safe place, or do I see it as a source of dangers?
- Where does that come from?
- How does it influence my style as a leader?
- How do I show up when I lead from a mindset of safety?
- How do I show up when I lead from a mindset of danger?
- Which one will serve me best in my current context and why?

Coaching the Different Mindsets and Beliefs

If you are reading this book, it's safe to assume that you are already interested and willing to Lead with Coaching as a key skill in your repertoire.

Coaching team members and even peers or colleagues taking into account their beliefs is already a "next level" commitment, because it will require you to go below the surface of your day-to-day transactional conversations, and to be ready to get out of your comfort zone in exploring more personal aspects of how they operate as leaders, potentially including some of their upbringing and personal context.

Here are some essential Dos and Don'ts to help you coach people based on their beliefs.

Dos:

- **Do take the time to learn more about them as individuals:** Be genuinely curious about their history growing up, their family structure, their peer relationships at school. This will help you have a good foundation to inform your perspective in terms of what are likely to be their dominant beliefs in each of the three key areas: collaboration vs. competition, scarcity vs. abundance, safety vs. danger.

- **Do observe them in their day-to-day interactions and behaviors:** They will give you hints in their leadership style that can allow you to have a hunch for what are likely to be their core beliefs, and it will help you make your own impressions for how that influences their actions, decisions, and choices.

- As you start exploring the role that beliefs play in how they show up as leaders, **do provide context for how beliefs usually influence how we lead,** and feel free to share some of your own findings from the self-reflection prompts we previously shared. For example, growing up in Argentina, I experienced both contexts of scarcity and abundance in big contrast, so it's relatively easy for me to pivot between mindsets when I lead, but I have to check myself every now and then to see if I am leading appropriately based on the specific context in which I am operating.

Don'ts:

- **Don't jump to conclusions:** Stay curious a little longer: if you have a hypothesis for how these beliefs might be influencing and informing their leadership style, stay in an exploratory mode through relevant "what" questions such as "What are some underlying assumptions you are making here when it comes to . . . ?" (collaboration, scarcity, risk-taking).

- **Don't assume without checking:** Check your hypothesis first with the person and feel free to call them up as a hunch if you are not sure. For example, you can say things like "knowing a bit about how you grew up as a track athlete, and having observed you recently in how you lead your team, I wonder if you are more naturally inclined to leading in contexts of competition and how that might influence how you show up if it's an environment where collaboration is required . . . how does that resonate with you?"

- **Don't be afraid to be wrong:** A lot of the work around beliefs can be very insightful to your coaching relationship, but there can also be gray zones. It's okay to test hypotheses as hunches, and sometimes if you get a strong reaction like "yes, that's totally me!" or even "no, that's not at all how I see the world . . . ," it will help you calibrate what really matters to the person you are coaching, and it will show them that you are listening and making an effort to go below the surface in understanding what drives them and how they operate.

Exercise: A Simple Coaching Framework to Examine Your Beliefs

In the spirit of practicing what we preach, it is important to understand the depth and origins of our belief systems, but sometimes you will be confronted with the need to do some "laser coaching" around specific beliefs that are getting in the way of you or your coachee achieving their goals, here and now.

You might not have the luxury of time to explore their personal background and the source of their beliefs, and you will feel the need to provide a practical and tactical approach to dealing with the impact of those beliefs in a more immediate way.

In these instances, the following framework will be a helpful go-to to help you coach your clients to examine, challenge, and shift their beliefs:

1. Think of the last time a belief held you back. What was the belief?

2. What impact did it have? What is the cost of holding this belief?

3. Digging into the belief:
   - Is it true?
   - Is it helpful?
   - Was it true once?
   - What is/was the source of this belief? (e.g., a person/a situation)

4. Going forward, decide what you want to do with this belief:
   - KEEP => because it's helpful
   - REVIEW AND AMMEND => so that it becomes useful
   - THROW AWAY => because it is untrue

As always, practice this framework in self-reflection first, or even better, enlist a friend or colleague to do it as a peer exercise. Reflect on your beliefs, and as you get to Step 4, deciding what to do with the belief, coach each other to develop an action plan to accept, refresh, or shift your beliefs.

"Beliefs drive behavior. And behavior determines the results you get in leadership."

—*Tony Robbins, Author and Speaker*

8

How Your Life Story IS Your Life Until Challenged

Beliefs are created in two ways. The first is through something you experienced yourself. The second is a belief that gets transferred to you by someone of influence over you at a certain time. Our values are created in much the same way. At the time that our beliefs and values were created, they clearly were valid to us and had merit to either help us or to protect us. However, with the passage of time, they can become outdated, and in later life with wisdom and understanding, we can then choose which ones to keep and which ones to abandon.

Despite being at the very core of our operating system, our beliefs often sit unnoticed in our subconscious mind, quietly influencing our thinking and behavior without us consciously knowing.

Our unconscious mind is also the vault that holds many of our values that also make a significant contribution to our unconscious operating system.

Sometimes, if someone asks us, we can articulate some of our beliefs and values, yet these responses are often colored by what we think we might be expected to say or the wish to give the right answer rather than the real answer. To uncover the real answers and indeed how our beliefs were formed, it is often helpful to listen carefully to someone's life story in such a way that allows the listener to interpret that person's beliefs and values.

It is only when we really understand our full beliefs and values system that we can become the fully authentic leader that is expected today. It is also only when we understand how these beliefs and values were created that we can decide which ones to keep because they genuinely help us personally or professionally and which ones to let go of because they do not help us and have become irrelevant since they were created.

A person's life story is absolutely not their resume. It is a recollection of the events and emotions that they remember vividly, mainly in the early part of their life; mainly from their first memory to around the time of puberty. This is when the mind is busy figuring out how the world works, how someone fits into their world order, and what could be deemed possible and desirable or impossible and either not desirable or downright painful and thus should be avoided.

Deconstructing Early Life Influences

If you allow me, I will use my own life story to demonstrate the power of understanding how one's early life influences our lives forever—until we audit it and decide, as adults, what we want to retain and what we want to let go. I will describe a series of situations, and then I will share with you the beliefs that were created at that time, and how they impacted my life and my leadership.

One of my first memories was, at about the age of three or four, being beside myself with excitement on my first plane flying with my mother and father to our new home in Malta. I distinctly remember the air hostess offering sweets on a silver tray. I had never seen so many sweets at one time, and I looked at my mother to see if I was really allowed to take one. She nodded. I took one and the hostess then said I could take as many as I wanted. I didn't dare take more than one.

The belief: That seemingly innocuous memory formed a deep belief in me that travel was highly desirable and very possible.

The impact of this belief on my leadership: This belief has guided my life ever since as I have navigated the world, worked, and lived, or at least visited, every continent and immersed myself in different cultures, languages, and experiences. As a professional leader and now as a coach, that has helped me to become extremely culturally adaptable and open to new and different experiences. These are important tenants for any coach. I am happy to retain these beliefs for the rest of my life.

When we arrived at our new home, my mother put me to bed and as she went to turn out the light she said "Oh, happy birthday darling." I pulled her toward me and asked her what she meant. She said that it had been my birthday that day but they had not wanted to tell me in case I was disappointed that it couldn't be celebrated while we were busy traveling. I was totally gutted. I couldn't understand how my parents had decided, in my mind, to deceive me and hide such an important piece of information from me. I had just turned four years old and didn't know that I had achieved such a remarkable milestone. I couldn't believe that my mother had hidden the truth from me.

The belief: I don't think I ever fully trusted my parents, or indeed others, to tell me the truth from that day on.

The impact of this belief on my leadership: I spent the rest of my life, until this process was done with me by a wonderful coach, trying to look around corners to see what I had not been told or what was being hidden from me. While this created a belief of suspicion it also created a strong value around my own honesty and my responsibility to tell what I see as the truth. This in turn has both served me well in many ways and sometimes has caused me to be too honest with occasional vicious consequences. I have reigned in the extremities of these now, which has been extremely helpful in my later life as a leader and as a coach.

Don't get me wrong, I was lucky enough to have been born to wonderful parents with good intentions and values. They were not to know that their four-year-old would interpret a "little white lie" in such an extreme way. They were doing the best they knew how and had no intention of hurting me or creating the belief of innate suspicion of the risk of using economic truth. This is true for many people whose parents fundamentally did their best for their children. Yet decisions often have unintended consequences.

My introverted father was a doctor and my extroverted mother an occupational therapist. Their professions gave them both a deep sense of responsibility that their life purpose was to be in service to others. My father would frequently get up in the middle of the night to go to tend to a patient, and I distinctly remember seeing a homeless person collapsed in the street one day. I observed how everyone walking on the street studiously avoided the body in the street. As soon as we approached my father knelt down to check the man's vital signs and put his finger in the man's mouth to ensure that his tongue was not obstructing his windpipe. He then put him in the recovery position and stopped someone who was trying to hurry past while looking in the opposite direction and literally commanded the person to call an ambulance.

The belief: This one was given to me, almost forced on me; I am here to be in service to others and their needs should come before my own.

The impact of this belief on my leadership: This has been both a rewarding and at times extremely challenging belief to live with, and one that I have had to learn to mitigate over time such that it is now a choice as to when I go with the belief and when I override it in the name of self-preservation. As a leader and as a coach, the concept of being in service to others is in fact at the very heart of what we should believe so this is one belief that I will hang on to more often than not.

Once I got to school I really struggled. I found learning to read and write extremely difficult and mathematics was like trying to read hieroglyphics. I was constantly bottom of the class, and there was an increasingly loud chorus from my teachers around my being both stupid and lazy. Yet I didn't feel stupid, I could see patterns and join dots that others could not. They were just not the patterns and dots that academics valued. In order to compensate for the stigma of being bottom of the class all the time, I learned how to be popular. I learned how to make people laugh and have fun together and how to help them when they were sad. I learned how to be a chameleon in all sorts of different social settings and how to read people and understand them in a way that others seemed incapable of divining. These were my survival techniques.

The belief: I knew early on that in order to prosper, I would have to forge my own path and that it would not be conventional. I had to believe in myself and trust that my way would see me through. These became my beliefs, forged out of necessity.

The impact of this belief on my leadership: This was highly annoying and deeply frustrating to my very academic father who would often vent his feelings about my apparent belligerence and rejection of the conventional. Yet I had to cling on to my belief that I would make it, because if I didn't and nobody else in my family did, then what?

Of course in time, it became clear that I was in fact extremely dyslexic rather than just sometimes stupid and lazy and yet here I am co-authoring my second book. My years as a commodity trader and then private equity professional allowed me, in terms of numbers, to trust in my ability to see patterns. I still transpose numbers, and they often look like spaghetti to me yet through the sea of noodles I can see where the opportunity lies in a set of numbers or where the mistake lies. I think that these experiences also contribute to my innate sense of optimism, which is also a strong belief—I believe that things will work out, and they usually do. I guess these beliefs have in fact served me well. I will keep them, and they have certainly helped me be a better leader and lifelong entrepreneur.

Another particularly vivid early memory for me was when my mother appeared as I was halfway through watching a documentary on grass snakes. She screamed and ran out of the room, reappearing minutes later with a broom that she used to turn the television off. At the time, I didn't know that she had a complete phobia of snakes born from a time in Sri Lanka when she was a young girl and went to put a plug into the bathtub when a huge cobra rose through the plug hole and watched her ominously while spreading its hood ready to strike. I was so shocked by my mother's screaming and the turning off of the TV with the broom that I too became phobic of snakes. Her belief was fully and successfully transferred to me.

The belief: I think it is obvious and is clearly unhelpful when making me paranoid about being bitten by a venomous snake while walking through snow.

The impact of this belief on my leadership: It may only have helped me as a coach to be a little more empathetic in terms of understanding that fear, real or perceived, can be debilitating. I will drop this belief, although I will always maintain a healthy respect for nature in all its forms.

So how have your beliefs shaped you? How does this understanding help you to lead others with coaching? We invite you to complete the following self-reflection exercise to experiment with this approach to distill beliefs from life experiences, and then examine how they have influenced your style and approach as a leader.

Exercise: Examining Your Beliefs

Self-Reflection: Think about the times in your early life that you can remember clearly and that had a profound emotional impact on you, and journal some of these experiences, similar to what we shared. Then:

- Think about how these may have contributed to the creation of your beliefs and values and how these show up in your daily leadership of others.
- Which beliefs were acquired through experience and which ones were someone else's that were transferred to you?
- Which of these beliefs help you, that you want to retain?
- How do they help you to be a better coach for your teams and the individuals in them?
- Which beliefs are less useful, or perhaps even hinder you, in your life and leadership today, that you want to let go of?

It is only through starting to understand your own life story and how that has influenced your beliefs and values that you can start to coach and help others to understand their beliefs and values and how they may help or hinder them.

This process of going through someone's life story may look daunting, especially as you then need to get the interpretation of what the story means in terms of someone else's beliefs and values. Leading with Coaching does not mean that you need to do this with each person that you are leading. It simply means that you can be aware of how these things can show up in your people.

You may simply observe how something connected to a belief or value is getting in the way of the potential of one of your people, and you may want to speak with them to investigate what makes them, for example, an eternal pessimist or an unrealistic optimist. You might ask in a 1:1 meeting something like "Do you remember something that you experienced in your early life that made you focus on the glass being half empty rather than half full?" A follow-up question might be "Given that some people find your pessimism demotivating, is there a way that you could develop a more balanced approach when speaking with the team?"

As you grow your coaching skills and get more comfortable with a coaching approach, you may one day want to do a full life story with someone. Often it is one of the most enlightening and revealing coaching approaches for the person telling their story and understanding its implications, usually for the first time in their lives.

If you do not feel comfortable to do this yet, do not rush it. Just think about what might be going on for someone that you, and possibly even they, are not aware of at a conscious level. Every single person has their own life story and every single life story has influenced that person profoundly whether they realize it or not. Each story has an impact on our behaviors on a daily basis, and they often affect our performance at work and our happiness in life so simply knowing a little about the subject helps you to lead with a coaching approach and mindset.

Looking Forward

In conclusion, there are hundreds of coaching frameworks, and they all help you essentially do the same thing: define a plan to go from your existing state (the present) to your desired state (the future), and the linchpin to this shift is forward momentum.

Many of these frameworks, including the ones we share in this book, can help you understand your current reality, develop and assess alternative paths of action, and create the engagement and commitment to make them a reality.

> *"Coaching is about helping clients unlock the treasure chest of their lives—worth bearing in mind then that diamonds are made from coal under pressure, and it's the grit in the oyster which creates the pearls."*
>
> *—Sarah Durran, Author*

9

Using Intuition as a Coach

In the business world there is often a tendency to value logic and reasoning over intuition. This is the result of many decades of dominant leadership styles that gave priority to IQ (Intellectual Quotient) over EQ (Emotional Quotient) traits, but we now know that both are equally important. In fact, research shows that as you grow in seniority and rank, once you have established your professional credibility on the bases of your reasoning, intellect, and functional expertise (your IQ), the single most powerful differentiator and driver of engagement and influence in your teams and in your environments is your ability to master the different components of EQ: self-awareness, self-regulation, social awareness, and relationship management.

Intuition plays a central role in all of these four areas because it allows people to navigate complex emotional landscapes with sensitivity, insight, and adaptability, leading to improved interpersonal relationships.

People often think that intuition is a nebulous concept, but as we know from the work of Malcom Gladwell in his book *Blink*, intuition is simply our cognitive ability to perform rapid subconscious processes that guide decision-making and problem-solving based on our accumulated experiences and pattern recognition. In other words, intuition is less of a "gut feeling" and much more of a "thin slicing" cognitive skill that can help us augment our ability to process subtle data such as body language, tone of voice, and contextual cues, that might be less obvious to pinpoint but that can be equally powerful in helping us interpret and respond accordingly.

Intuition is a key skill for leaders who want to strengthen their EQ as they coach others, because it can help build:

- **Emotional Perception**: Intuition helps in perceiving and understanding emotions accurately, both in yourself and others. This is how we are capable of picking up on subtle signs such as body language, tone of voice, and facial expressions, which are crucial for interpreting emotions when we coach others.

- **Empathy**: Intuition plays a vital role in developing empathy, which is the ability to understand and share the feelings of others. Through intuition, leaders that want to be good coaches can sense the emotions underlying someone's words or actions, enabling them to respond with empathy and compassion.

- **Decision-making**: Intuition can guide decision-making, especially in emotionally charged situations, helping us consider not just logical elements but also emotional ones, leading to more balanced and thoughtful decisions. Good coaches that understand intuition can help coachees unpack their decision-making criteria to dissect the role that emotions are playing in their process.

- **Social Skills**: Intuition enhances social skills by helping us understand social dynamics and navigate interpersonal relationships. It helps individuals gauge the emotional climate of a situation and adapt their behavior accordingly, fostering positive interactions and collaboration.

Great coaches rely on intuition to guide their work with clients. We often refer to it as "taking the plunge" when we call out what we see in our clients, because we trust that what we know, what we sense, and what we observe are a reflection of our client's inner experience that is getting manifested in the different layers of their behavior: their pace, their demeanor, a shift in their energy and tone are great cues for our intuition to pick up signs of what is beyond what is being said in words.

In order to create space to develop and further fine-tune your intuition as a coach to fellow leaders, here are a few self-reflection prompts that can help you examine the role that intuition plays in your personal and professional life. The more attuned you are with your natural intuition, the more helpful you will be as a leader-coach.

SELF-REFLECTION PROMPTS:

- What is my definition of intuition in my own words?
- What is my personal score of 1–10 for how much I use and trust my intuition in my life as a leader (where 1 is "I don't use or trust my intuition at all," and 10 is "I rely heavily on my intuition as a leader")?
- Considering my current level of trust in my intuition, has it changed over time? If so, why?
- When was a time that I trusted my intuition and it led to a positive outcome? Describe that experience in detail.

- When did I ignore my intuition and then regret it? What did I learn from that experience?

- How do I distinguish between intuition and other forms of decision-making, such as logic or emotions?

- What are my fears or doubts about relying on intuition? What are the sources of these fears, and how could they impact the work I want to do in coaching others?

- What challenging decision am I currently facing? How am I incorporating my intuition into the process?

- How do I nurture and develop my intuition? Are there practices or habits that can help me tap into my intuitive sense more effectively?

"Effective leaders are alike in one crucial way: they all have a high degree of what has come to be known as emotional intelligence. It's not that IQ and technical skills are irrelevant. They do matter, but . . . they are the entry-level requirements for executive positions."

—*Daniel Goleman, Bestselling Author*

One-to-One Coaching

Even though executive and leadership coaching have many facets and formats, when people think of coaching, the first thing that comes to mind is 1:1 coaching, as it's the "bread and butter" of this wonderful discipline. In fact, most coaching definitions implicitly describe the nature of a process between two people:

- **International Coach Federation (ICF):** "Executive coaching is partnering with clients in a thought-provoking and creative process that inspires them to maximize their personal and professional potential."

- **European Mentoring & Coaching Council (EMCC):** "Executive coaching is a professional service that supports individuals in leadership roles to become more effective. It involves a collaborative, solutions-focused, results-orientated and systematic process in which the coach facilitates the enhancement of work performance, life experience, self-directed learning and personal growth of the coachee."

- **Harvard Business Review:** "Executive coaching is an experiential and individualized leader development process that builds a leader's capability to achieve short- and long-term organizational goals."

- **Center for Creative Leadership (CCL):** "Executive coaching is a confidential, one-on-one relationship between a coach and a leader. It is focused on enhancing the leader's capability to achieve short- and long-term organizational goals and to develop the leader's own skills and behaviors."

Ultimately, 1:1 coaching is a Thinking Partnership between two people, where the coach guides a process of questions and inquiry that helps the coachee find their own answers and solutions.

So to get to that goal, you need to first understand what it takes to get two people to build a Thinking Partnership. It takes a tiered approach. The first step is the willingness of one person to ask another person to help them think something through as a partner.

We call this the HELP model: we often ask our clients "What do you think most people feel most of the time when they have to ask for help?" What we hear is always along the lines of:

- Embarrassed
- Incompetent
- Ashamed
- Stupid
- Vulnerable
- Exposed

Then we ask them: "How do you feel when someone asks you for a few moments of your time to help them think something through?" And then we invariably hear that they felt:

- Trusted
- Valued
- Resourceful
- Competent
- Respected
- Appreciated
- Connected

What an interesting contrast, right? How often do we hold back from asking for help because of fear of our own negative feelings, when in fact when we ask for help we are giving someone the gift of feeling valued, respected, trusted, and purposeful. All it takes is our willingness to ask an incredibly simple yet profoundly powerful question:

Could you please help me think something through together?

This is at the heart of creating Thinking Partnerships: our willingness and ability to collaborate with someone through a structured process of deliberate questions that create the insight and action to help them get to their goals.

Trilogy Questions©: The Secret Sauce to Effective Thinking Partnerships

As we have shared in the previous chapters, good questions are the engine of good coaching. But like with anything "simple," there's a real art and science when it comes to asking the right question, at the right time, in the right way.

Our approach to this is what we call "Trilogy Questions," which is simply asking the following questions:

- What do I want?
- How will I get it?
- Who needs to be involved/When is the outcome expected?

These are simple questions, but the real power comes from the fact that each of them is actually the first prompt to a much deeper set of deliberate and intentional questions. And here's where the "art and science" comes, in how much time we spend exploring each of these three areas, and how we frame the questions.

1. What Do I Want?

When we work with clients, and especially in a strategic business environment, we often realize that people get in their own way because they have a tendency to jump straight into the HOW, without having created fundamental alignment and clarity at the WHAT level: what is going on, what does success look like, what have we done so far, what have we learned. If you are missing alignment and clarity in these areas, there is simply no way to get to a good HOW! That's why the sequence of starting with WHAT and staying in it for much longer than you typically would (up to 60% of your time) is the first golden rule of Trilogy Questions (see Figure 10.1).

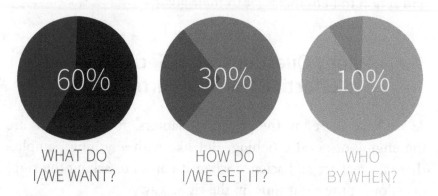

FIGURE 10.1 The Trilogy Questions Structure

Here are some of our best WHAT questions to help you structure your Thinking Partnerships:

- What is going on, in a nutshell?
- What does success look like?
- What does "good" look like?
- What have we done so far?
- What has worked, what has not worked?
- What have we learned?
- What is holding us back?
- What is the impact on the team/the business?
- What do we know for sure, and what don't we know? What is the impact of not knowing?
- What data do we have? What data do we need?
- What is a realistic view of the issue?
- What is our best thinking about this so far?
- What is the level of urgency to act on this? What's driving it?
- What is the impact of doing nothing?
- What are we underestimating?
- What should we START doing?
- What should we STOP doing?
- What are the skills/thinking style that we need to work on this?
- Who are our stakeholders, and what is the impact on them?

Needless to say, you don't need to ask every question in every Thinking Partnership. As an experienced leader, you need to use your knowledge and best judgment to select those that are most relevant to the issue at hand, and as you build your muscle in asking good WHAT questions, you will even build your own list of "greatest hits" and go-to questions for impact.

2. How Will I Get It?

Once you have created real clarity and alignment at the WHAT level, the HOW follows through with real ease, because a lot of the actions that you will explore will be highly connected to the insights you identified during the previous stage.

Some of our best HOW questions include:

- What are all the possible solutions?
- What is the best game plan you see?
- What support/resources do we need?
- On a scale of 1–10, how realistic is this plan?
- What strengths can we leverage?
- How will we engage our stakeholders?
- What can derail us? How do we mitigate the risk of these derailers?
- How will we know when we achieved our goal?
- How will we feel when we've achieved our goal?
- How can we sustain our goal?
- On a scale of 1–10, how badly do we want this?
- What progress do we want to see in the next week/month?
- What will be the signs that we are on track/off track? What will be the early yellow flags?

Who Needs to Be Involved/When Is the Outcome Expected?

As you can see, HOW questions are simpler and to the point because we want to help get into action, explore options, and build forward momentum. The next stage of Trilogy Questions is all about creating commitment and ownership for next steps in terms of WHO and WHEN.

Some of our best questions for this last stage include:

- What is the first step we need to take?
- What are the following steps?
- What is a quick win?
- What is the time frame for these steps?
- Who will do what by when?
- What do we want the situation to look like a year from now?
- On a scale of 1–10, how committed are we?

By now, as you followed these steps through the discipline and depth of the questions, you will have created:

1. Clarity about what is going on in the current state
2. Alignment on what success looks like
3. Options for ideas to address the needs/challenges
4. Actions to walk the talk
5. Commitment to take ownership of the actions
6. A concrete plan to make it happen

In essence, Trilogy Questions are a coaching framework to structure, simplify, and focus on how you think about complex and challenging issues in Thinking Partnerships. The more you practice these frameworks, the more natural it will become for you to be in the zone of coaching.

As we have learned through our decades of working with clients, experts may have the answers, but the best leaders leverage coaching as the art and science of asking great questions, because that helps people take ownership of the actions that come from them, having co-created the right answers in partnership, as opposed to just being told what to do.

TIPS TO COACH USING TRILOGY QUESTIONS

- Give your client a bit of background to the framework and its format before you start bringing it to life, so that they start noticing the process as you go through it. This will help them "learn by doing" and will allow them to practice it independently and in their day-to-day.

- Spend WAY more time than you typically would at the WHAT level and don't move into the HOW unless you feel you have really created clarity and alignment.

- Invite your client to also ask good quality WHAT questions, to practice the premise as they get coached

- Welcome their own exploration to areas where they want to go deeper, and as you see them thinking and processing, do prompt "what question would you ask yourself here?," to help them get comfortable with the idea of self-coaching.

Beware: "Why" Is a Four-Letter Word in Coaching

If you have worked with an experienced coach, you may have noticed that we avoid asking questions that start with "why." It's a somewhat secret tool of the trade, to the point that even the International Coaching Federation (ICF) has this recommendation as part of its coaching guidelines and certification standards.

We advise avoiding questions that start with "why" for several reasons:

- It creates defensiveness: "Why" questions can make the person being asked feel judged or attacked. "Why" questions can make people feel they need to justify their actions, leading to a defensive or emotional reaction. They might interpret the question as a challenge or an accusation, which can shut down open communication and create defensiveness and barriers to honest dialogue. In fact, brain studies by the National Institutes of Health (NIH) have shown that asking "why" questions can sometimes trigger emotional responses, activating the amygdala, which processes emotions like fear and defensiveness.

- It puts the focus on the past: "Why" questions often focus on previous actions or decisions, which can lead to dwelling on what went wrong and what one's role was in it, rather than looking forward to solutions and future actions. This past-focused perspective limits the exploration of a situation to just the history and reasoning behind it, rather than exploring broader possibilities and perspectives going into the future.

Instead, coaches prefer to use questions that start with "what" or "how" because they tend to be more open-ended and forward focused. These types of questions encourage exploration, reflection, and action, helping clients to think creatively and consider various solutions. For example:

- "What led you to make that decision?"
- "How did you feel about the outcome?"
- "What could you do differently next time?"
- "How can you approach this situation going forward?"

These questions and all others we shared in the Trilogy Questions© framework are designed to facilitate deeper thinking and self-awareness, fostering a more productive and supportive coaching conversation.

Case Study: Transforming Leadership Through a Coaching Mindset

By Janet Miller Evans, Executive Coach

Susan, a leader known for her brilliance and decisiveness, faced a challenge. Despite her unmatched ability to produce high-quality work and make tough decisions, she was experiencing tension with her colleagues and team members. The feedback she received was a mix of admiration for her capabilities and concern about her communication style and interpersonal interactions. However, after Susan transformed her leadership approach by adopting a coaching mindset, the feedback she received was overwhelmingly positive, instilling hope in her and her team for a more effective and harmonious future.

When Susan first joined her team, her confidence and decisiveness were immediately apparent. She was objective and always seemed to know the right answer. However, as she quickly immersed herself in the new environment, some of her colleagues began to feel that she was too opinionated. They thought she sometimes jumped to conclusions without fully understanding the context, making her appear to lack substance.

Additionally, Susan's communication style was often perceived as abrupt and brusque. Her written emails were all business, without warmth or friendliness, and she rarely smiled or turned on her camera on Zoom calls. This gave her an air of aloofness, making it difficult for her colleagues to connect with her on a personal level.

Moreover, Susan's rapid speech and quick judgments often gave the impression that she wanted to end conversations as quickly as possible. Some team members even felt she had a chip on her shoulder, which manifested in a strident attitude and demeanor toward others.

Realizing the need for change, Susan made a crucial decision. She understood that her technical skills and decisiveness, while valuable, were not enough to lead effectively in the dynamic organizational culture. She needed to develop a more nuanced approach—one that would allow her to connect and build trust.

Susan decided to embrace a coaching mindset and leadership style, focusing on active listening, powerful questioning, and emotional intelligence. This shift in perspective would require her to refine her communication skills and develop a more empathetic and supportive approach to leadership.

First, Susan slowed down and began listening to her colleagues. She started paying more attention during meetings. Instead of quickly offering her opinions, she began asking clarifying questions to ensure she understood their perspectives.

In one instance, instead of jumping to a conclusion about a problem during a team discussion, she asked, "This situation seems unusual. What experiences do you have with similar issues, and how did you handle them?" This simple shift in approach encouraged her team to share their insights and fostered a more collaborative atmosphere.

Susan also started using more open-ended questions in her interactions. She realized that by asking questions like "What are your thoughts on this?" or "How do you think we should approach this problem?" she could encourage her team members to think critically and contribute meaningfully to discussions.

(continued)

(*continued*)

For example, instead of immediately stating her opinion on a challenge during a project meeting, she asked her team, "What options do we have to address this? How do we evaluate which one is the best?" This approach empowered her team to take ownership of the solution and demonstrated her willingness to consider their ideas.

Susan knew that to be a more effective leader, she needed to develop her emotional intelligence. She began by making a concerted effort to understand her colleagues' backgrounds and experiences. This helped her show greater empathy and avoid making assumptions about others' experiences.

When a colleague mentioned he was going on vacation, Susan took the opportunity to engage in a more personal conversation. "That sounds great! Where are you planning to go? I hope you have a relaxing time," she said, showing genuine interest. This small act of kindness helped soften her image and made her more approachable.

Recognizing the importance of face-to-face communication, Susan started initiating more phone calls and turning on her video during Zoom meetings. She also made it a point to smile more and include some light conversation at the start of meetings to create a warmer, more inviting atmosphere.

Regular check-ins became a part of her routine. She began asking her team members about their well-being and how she could support them in their work. "How is your current project going? Is there any way I can assist you?" The regular engagement built trust and made her team feel more valued and supported.

Susan saw a great opportunity to practice her new approach with Sheila, the new office manager. She decided to act as a mentor, offering guidance and support with kindness. Whenever Sheila encountered difficulties, Susan would say, "I understand this task is challenging. How can I support you in overcoming these obstacles?"

By focusing on empathy, patience, and understanding, Susan helped Sheila grow in her role while also enhancing her own leadership capabilities.

Over time, Susan's efforts began to pay off. Her colleagues noticed a significant change in her demeanor and approach. She now demonstrated a willingness to listen, an openness to new ideas, and a genuine interest in the well-being of her team. The feedback from her team became more positive, highlighting her ability to lead with empathy and support while maintaining her strengths in decision-making and quality of work.

Susan's transformation into a coaching leader not only improved her relationships with her colleagues but also led to a more collaborative team. By embracing a coaching mindset, Susan created a more cooperative and positive work environment, ultimately contributing to her organization's success.

The Performance Equation

Part of Leading with Coaching is knowing how to develop people and teams, identifying what is valued in the workplace today and what will be valued in the future. In this respect, we are experiencing rapid and irrevocable change. In the recent past, know-how, skills, and knowledge held the highest value—people were paid to be experts in their field. With the advent of ever more powerful search engines and now generative artificial intelligence in many fields, knowledge has become a downloadable commodity. Even in spheres such as medicine, AI has as much or more diagnostic capability as your doctor and the balance is tipping rapidly. This means that what has traditionally been valued is a declining currency. So what skills are on the ascendence?

In short, leadership and especially the type of leadership that takes people through unchartered change. Almost every business we work with is undergoing a transformation of their business model or their use of technology as a future enabler, or both. It is ironic in this context to note that so many people are hardwired to resist change. Many don't like moving from understanding to exploration of the unknown. Many leaders find it uncomfortable to answer a question with the honest response of "I don't know." Our initial resistance to change is eroded once we see the benefit of that change. In other words, our attitude to a particular change moves us from resistance to acceptance.

So much of the coaching that you will do as a leader will be around how people can adopt a mindset or attitude that helps them to accept change faster, that allows them to lead people through uncertainty, that makes them accessible, authentic, and helpful to others through the change process. This means that the new equation of performance weights attitude far more than capability, as you can see in Figure 10.2.

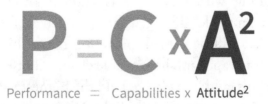

$$P = C \times A^2$$

Performance = Capabilities x Attitude²

FIGURE 10.2 The Performance Equation

Of course, people are still expected to have a minimum set of capabilities in the workplace. But their biggest business driver now and into the future will be their attitude, which is the reason it is squared in the performance equation.

NOTE: Attitude is our single biggest performance driver.

There can be no doubt that how we think about something can alter the outcome we achieve. We know that if we think about how good we will feel at the end of our gym session that we are more likely to go to the gym and enjoy our workout than if we focus on how hard it will be to do the workout. We know that how we think about a travel delay can quickly lead us to either accepting the delay and perhaps visiting the book shop to browse for our next best read or lead us into anger and catastrophic fantasies about the consequence of the delay and who we are going to complain to.

We know that a gold medal Olympian is physically much the same as a silver medal Olympian so could it be that it is the gold medalist's attitude that makes the difference?

Very few business people spend time every day choosing their attitude toward the day, the challenge ahead, or the performance challenge they face. Much of a leader's coaching approach needs to be around what attitude can help someone's performance and what attitude is unhelpful to that person's performance or the performance of those working with that individual.

Before coaching someone else on their attitude, think about how you set your own.

SELF-REFLECTION PROMPTS:

- How often do I choose my attitude to a challenge?
- What is my attitude on a good day versus my attitude on a bad day?

- When I consciously decide to adopt an attitude that I think will help me, how does it affect the outcome I achieve?
- How can I make it part of my daily routine to choose my attitude?

Thinking about the people you are leading, think how you can coach them to think about their attitudes—which are helpful and which are not. Perhaps share the performance equation with them to prompt them to be more aware of their attitude and the fact that very often it is, or can be, their biggest performance driver. Remind them that attitude affects all interactions and thought processes and that, so long as we are in good mental health, we really can choose our attitude. Encourage them to choose wisely.

"A coach is someone who tells you what you don't want to hear, who has you see what you don't want to see, so you can be who you have always known you could be."

—Tom Landry, Hall of Fame NFL Coach

11

The Art of Self-Determination: Deciding on My Way of Being

Your attitude is just part of how you decide on your way of being. In other words: we fly our own plane. We all have that voice in our head that chatters to us a remarkable amount of each day. Often it seems that our inner voice is intent on sabotaging us. It asks us questions like "why is it always *my* plane that gets delayed?" This is clearly a fallacy as many planes all over the world get delayed every day. Yet the question our inner voice asks leads us to answer it—most often leading us rapidly into victimhood, a bad mood, or even into an angry state. Had we noticed that inner thought, we could have changed the question to deliver a better way of being, such as "how can I make this delay, over which I have no control, into a benefit?"

NOTE: We tend not to acknowledge that we do actually control, if we choose to, our inner voice and that we can retrain it to become much more helpful to us. It can make us more resilient, more content, and less stressed.

It is important to stress that the point here is not to ignore the way we are in the immediate moment. We cannot skip from a negative state of mind to a positive state of mind at will and we certainly cannot do that without first acknowledging our initial inner state. The point is to ask ourselves whether that initial inner state will help us or not. If the answer is that it will not be helpful, then we have the choice to choose a different inner state. We have to go through this process, as trying to jump from a negative state to a positive state without first acknowledging our starting point is likely to feel very artificial and inauthentic and is therefore unlikely to work.

This takes careful and conscious observation, and it takes time. The more stressed we are the less able we are to objectively observe our thought patterns and the speech patterns of our inner voice. For many people, the neuropathways used by our inner voice are deeply entrenched and therefore take repetitive effort to reroute and reengineer. Yet it is work entirely worth doing as the rewards, both big and small, become so evident and make our thoughts, feelings, and behaviors so much better that it can literally be life enhancing.

Beware the Overuse of Humility

Humility is sometimes our friend and sometimes our enemy. Many people find it easier and more acceptable to dwell on our failures, our insecurities, and our fears rather than giving equal credence to our strengths, our individual superpowers, and our life navigation skills. As a coach, use authentic praise when it is due as a way to balance someone's humility with their confidence. Very often we learn faster through praise, as we would like it to be repeated, than we do from "constructive" (negative) feedback.

SELF-REFLECTION PROMPTS:

- How does my inner voice speak to me?
- Do I let it decide what it says to me or do I take conscious control of it so that it becomes helpful?
- What is the difference between how it speaks to me on a good day versus a bad day?
- What would a continuously helpful voice sound like and what positive questions, thoughts, feelings, and behaviors would it enable?
- What questions would that helpful voice ask and what else would it say to me?
- What negative questions do I want my inner voice to stop asking?
- How can I retrain my inner voice to be more helpful more often?

Over to You, Coach

Now think about those you work with. How do you think their inner voices sound to them? How could you help them to take proactive control over their inner voice such that it became far more constructive to them? For example, you could ask, what is your inner voice saying to you right now? Is that helpful to you? If not, let's use the Trilogy Questions structure to capture what would be most helpful to you, how you can shift to that way of being, and when you can make the change. We all know that the words we use with other people matter yet we rarely audit the words we use on ourselves to check whether they are empowering and enabling or an extremely subtle form of self-sabotage. As a coach, your job is to help people choose.

Helping people access memories can also be very powerful in enabling them to decide their way of being. Imagine a member of your team is discernably nervous about a task ahead of them. Ask them how they are feeling and what they are thinking in terms of getting this task done. If they were to say that they are afraid that they cannot do it or that they lack the confidence to get it done, just acknowledge their thoughts and feelings. Then ask them to think of a time when they overcame their fears or lack of confidence and succeeded in completing a challenge that initially seemed daunting. Ask them to remember how they moved from daunted to determined and thereby achieved success. Finally ask them if what helped them last time would help them this time and if so, how they can make the shift to help them get the current task done successfully.

Obedient Minds

It is quite remarkable that our unconscious minds are entirely obedient. What we mean by that is that our brain answers the questions it is asked. So, to take an extreme example, if we ask someone what they are afraid of and what they will find most difficult about the task ahead of them, they will answer the questions posed. If, on the other hand, we ask someone what they are excited about and how their past experiences will help them with the task ahead of them, then they will answer those questions instead. This is, quite literally, how we set the mind and hence the word mindset. Leading with Coaching is very often about helping people achieve the right mindset. Think about the people you lead and how you can help them adopt a mindset that will feed their success.

Help them choose their way of being.

"Don't let the noise of others' opinions drown out your own inner voice. And most importantly, have the courage to follow your heart and intuition."

—*Steve Jobs, Founder of Apple*

12

The Power of Visualization

The art of self-determination can be greatly enhanced by the science and the practice of visualization.

There are two things that professional athletes would never live without. One is a coach and the other is the skill of visualization. Yet in the work context we very rarely use the skill of visualization.

The Business of Sport: See It, Feel It

Anyone who has ever played any form of sport knows how important visualization is. In tennis, we know when we have taken a good shot before the ball ever has contact with our racket. This is because we have rehearsed the shot in our mind in preparation as the ball heads toward us. We know where we are aiming our return, we know how high or low we want the ball to go and we know what a good backhand or forehand "feels" like before we ever hit the ball. Skiing is much the same. We get to the top of a slope, and we look down, planning our route, thinking where to make our turns, knowing how it will feel to navigate the slope well. We literally see and feel our descent ahead of our first move.

Sports coaches train athletes to visualize everything they do before they do it, whether that is taking aim at a goal, hitting the baseball for a home run, or aiming the basketball at the net.

This prepares us both mentally and physically. It allows the mind to ready itself for what lies ahead and to calibrate how it feels while we are actually doing something versus how it should have felt when we visualized it. When it doesn't feel as it should, when we feel that we are skiing down a slope with less control than we anticipated, it provides us with an opportunity to stop, reassess, and revisualize such that we can start again, grounded and ready, perhaps with a slightly different approach based on our latest understanding of conditions such as visibility or ice.

We can use the same techniques in our day-to-day lives and especially in preparation for what we have to do in the context of our work. Much of coaching someone is also about helping the person to visualize themselves doing something successfully.

Carpe Diem

One of the best leaders we have ever worked with has turned the art of visualization into a science that is now completely embedded in his routine. Each morning, he makes a cup of coffee and sits in silence looking out at his garden. He notices his mood. He gauges whether he has slept enough and what impact that is likely to have on his energy levels at certain times during the day. Having looked at his diary the night before he can see the sequence of meetings and interactions that he has ahead of him for the day. He can picture each meeting and many of the people he will see during the day.

Having checked his state of mind, he asks himself the first of the Trilogy Questions: What do I want today to be like? What do I want people to experience from interactions with me today? What level of energy and presence would most help me and others to have a good day today?

He visualizes each of the answers to these questions, picturing himself in his meetings as if he were observing himself as a third-party observer. Once he is clear as to what good looks like and feels like, he moves to the second of the Trilogy Questions: How can I achieve a good day today, given my mood, my energy levels, my mindset. If he is tired and low in energy, he acknowledges that and then focuses on how to improve those things and how much better he will feel when he has consciously mastered getting the best result possible in the given circumstances. Once he is clear on his "how" for the day, he answers "me" to the third of the Trilogy Questions—Who/When—me, as of now.

When we introduced this way of starting his day to him, he balked at the time it would take out of his already busy days. It would take him about 15 minutes to go through the whole visualization. Today, it often takes him less than five minutes to complete and, once done, he is full of the purpose of his day.

Many of his colleagues noted that there had been a real shift in his demeanor once he started to use this technique and they asked him how he managed to be so upbeat, so present, and so consistent in his approach to meetings regardless of them covering good or bad news. So, he started sharing his morning routine with his team and asking them early in the day if they had done their visualization that morning and if so how they were feeling. Over a period of time, having coached his team on how to do this, they all noticed how much better their team meetings went and how much more they got done.

They also felt better, more able to choose their way of being, and more likely to have a good day, no matter the challenges.

SELF-REFLECTION:

Try these visualization techniques for yourself and if you like the results you get, share them with your team members.

Visualizing for Public Speaking: How to Tame Your Performance Anxiety

Many people find public speaking daunting. For some it can create severe anxiety. However, you can really help people overcome their fears with some good presentation coaching that uses visualization as a core tool. Coaching your team to do awesome presentations is one of the great opportunities of Leading with Coaching, primarily because it makes the people you lead look great and also because the better the talent you lead is perceived, the better you look, too.

Presentation coaching is a process so let's go through it step by step.

Step One: Content

Good presentations are good stories, told well. Walk the person you are coaching through the Emotional Leadership Framework in Chapter 6 so as to give the content the optimal flow that engages the audience's hearts and minds. It is important, even at the early stages of crafting a story, to keep in mind what your audience wants to know, how you want them to respond to the presentation, and how you want them to feel about you and the story at the end of the presentation.

Although a presentation should not be more than around 10 slides and last no more than 20 minutes, ask the person you are coaching to write the script for the presentation before even attempting to write the slides. The script needs to be in the voice of the presenter to ensure maximum authenticity and to allow their enthusiasm for the topic to be evident.

Once the script is written, it can be timed to ensure that it is not too long, checked to be sure the key messages for the audience are clear and that the tone is one that the audience will relate to; then the slides can be prepared.

Step Two: Practice, Practice

Once the script is written, it needs to be practiced over and over again—preferably in front of a mirror. The advantage of this is that the presenter is seeing themselves as the audience will. It helps focus on eye contact, on looking and feeling relaxed and it develops the familiarity with the content that will allow the script to be discarded eventually for prompt cards with only the key bullets on them as reminders of the flow in case the presenter gets lost or freezes at any point.

Once the prompt cards are written, they can be used in conjunction with the original script for yet more practice in front of the mirror. At this point, the presenter should be feeling pretty confident that the content is known to them, and they can start to practice the speed of delivery, at what points to pause for effect and how to use their hands and eye contact to emphasize particular points. We would always recommend that practice be done at least once at night so that the brain can sleep on it.

Step 3: Visualize

While practicing, encourage the presenter to visualize the audience, to visualize their own confidence in their delivery, and to picture the audience showing their attention, interest, and engagement to both the content of the presentation and, even more importantly, to the person presenting. Ask the presenter to imagine what the audience would say to each other at the end of the presentation if it was brilliantly delivered.

And ask them to describe how they would feel if they knew that they were doing a great job presenting with confidence, warmth, and knowledge. Listen carefully to how they describe themselves at their best and do not hurry the process—let them deeply imagine their most successful state.

SELF-REFLECTION:

Some good coaching questions that might help the visualization process include:

- How would you feel if you were presenting at your best?
- When you are at your most confident, how do you feel and what goes through your mind?
- Knowing that you are well prepared, how can you ensure that you relax and enjoy the process of presenting?
- Do you use any breathing techniques to help calm your nerves before you present?
- How would you feel at the end of the presentation if you overheard someone in the audience say to their neighbor "That was a great presentation"?

Looking Forward

There are innumerable circumstances where we can use visualization in a work context. We can use it to plan client meetings, we can use it for project management, team meetings, stakeholder management, patient interaction, career planning, negotiation, and almost any type of meeting or interaction with other people.

Note that when we use the term *visualization*, we refer to it in its broadest sense. Some people are not very visual, so they may want to focus more on how success makes them feel. Others are more auditory and may prefer to think in terms of what they sound like at their best. Whatever form of their imagination is most accessible to them can be used for the purpose of visualization.

As the coach of your people, help them get into the habit of using this transformational technique to help them reach the best of their potential.

"Whatever your mind can conceive and believe, it can achieve."

—*Napoleon Hill, Author*

13

The Importance of Values in Leadership and Coaching

Values are essential to all of us, because they calibrate our compass to set our true north and establish our direction. As leaders, our values guide us in good and bad times: what matters most, how we make decisions, and how we deal with challenges—it's all heavily influenced by our values.

Our values can be shaped by various factors including culture, upbringing, religion, education, and personal experiences, and even though we have a set of core values that tends to remain at our core throughout life, they can evolve over time. Some values become more important, others less, and we can incorporate new ones as our worldview and experiences get richer and deeper.

Therefore, revisiting and refreshing your values every few years can be a very helpful exercise, because it can help you crystalize insights and adjust how you operate both in your personal and professional life as a result of your values.

When it comes to coaching, values are of deep importance because a good coach needs to adapt their style and approach to what's important to their client. Values are particularly influential in a coaching relationship because they are core to your client's direction, identity, and motivation:

- **Direction:** Values provide a moral compass that helps individuals navigate life's challenges and make decisions consistent with their beliefs and principles.

- **Identity:** Values define who individuals are and what they stand for, shaping their self-concept, purpose, and worldview.

- **Motivation:** Values influence motivation and behavior by determining what individuals consider meaningful and worthwhile pursuits. People are more likely to be motivated when their actions align with their values, and they tend to get stuck when they don't.

In an ideal world, our values and our actions should always align. But in the real world, there are often situations in which the context has a set of challenges that will test us. For example, sometimes leaders that have fairness and merit as core values will struggle if the business culture in which they operate tends to pick favorites based on personal preferences. In these cases, the person will have an inner struggle to reconcile what matters to them, with how they should operate as a leader in that environment.

When your values and your actions are not aligned, it can lead to a variety of consequences, both internal and external:

- **Internal conflict:** A sense of dissonance, with feelings of guilt, shame, or dissatisfaction when your behavior contradicts what you believe to be right or important.

- **Emotional distress**: Acting in ways that are inconsistent with your values can cause anxiety, stress, or frustration. When not resolved, if these feelings are intense and persist over time, they might even contribute to burnout.

- **Loss of authenticity**: When you prioritize external expectations or societal norms over your own values, you may lose a sense of authenticity and personal integrity and undermine your sense of identity.

- **Decreased motivation and fulfillment**: Pursuing goals that do not align with your values can make you feel demotivated or uninspired, leading to a sense of emptiness or stagnation in your personal or professional life.

- **Incongruence in decision-making**: When your actions are not guided by your values, you may make decisions that are inconsistent or irrational.

Therefore, as coaches, it's key that at the beginning of establishing a coaching relationship we spend time seeing the world through the lens of our client's values.

> *"Great leaders don't just focus on the bottom line. They start with their values and inspire others to do the same. When values guide decisions, leadership becomes a force for good."*
>
> —*Simon Sinek, Author*

Time to Practice on Yourself

In order to explore and understand your values, the following self-reflection exercise can help crystalize what's most important, how you are living in alignment with their values (or not), and what kind of shifts you need to make in order to align your actions and values.

Please take the time to complete this exercise yourself first, as it will give you a good sense of the process that your coachees will follow, and it will also give you some insight into your own values and choices as they stand today.

Exercise: Values Alignment

As a leader, it's important to regularly practice "self-reflection" in order to remain clear about who you are, what you stand for, what you believe, and what you care most about. This clarity guides you through the many challenges, decisions, and conflicts you face as a leader and helps you to operate authentically. This "values alignment" exercise helps you reflect on your most important values and how well your life is aligned with your most important values.

Part I

The first part of this exercise asks you to prioritize your values by rank ordering the list (1–20, with 1 being the most important value). It requires careful thought to complete the rank ordering. You are not to concern yourself in this section with what your values "wish list" is but rather what your true priorities are. These priorities can change over your lifetime, which is why it's important to do this exercise when major changes happen in your life or when you haven't done this for quite some time.

Importance Rank 1–20	Value Description
	Location: To be able to live and work where I want to be
	Creativity: To be innovative; to create new and better ways of doing things

Importance Rank 1–20	Value Description
	Wealth: To earn a great deal of money (well beyond my family's basic needs)
	Independence: To have the freedom to act on my own terms, without direction from others
	Power: To have the authority over the activities and careers of others; including allocation of people and resources
	Security: To financially meet my family's needs without having to worry
	Balance: To balance my work interests with outside interests to experience total personal satisfaction
	Health: To be physically and mentally fit
	Prestige: To be recognized by others as being successful. To be well known in my chosen field
	Personal Growth: To continue to grow in my self-awareness; continue to do challenging work that utilizes my talents and to evolve as a human being
	Loyalty: To be committed to the goals of a team who share my beliefs, values, and ethical principles
	Purpose: To do things that really matter, with a deeper meaning and a long-lasting impact above and beyond my own reality
	Family: To spend time with family members and create cherished memories
	Friendship: To have people in my life whom I enjoy spending time with, whom I care about and respect (at work and outside of work)
	Leadership: To motivate and energize a group of people toward a common goal and demonstrate responsibility for identifying and accomplishing our goals and mission

(continued)

(continued)

Importance Rank 1–20	Value Description
	Integrity: To live and work in alignment with my moral standards; to be honest and stand up for my beliefs
	Achievement: To achieve significant goals, whether they bring me recognition from others or not
	Recognition: To receive acknowledgment and affirmation for my contributions
	Service: To contribute to the well-being of others who need help; to help improve society
	Wisdom: To grow in understanding of my personal calling; to find lasting meaning in what I do
	. . . . [If a core value you hold essential is missing, feel free to add it.]

Part II

1. List your top five values from Part I in order of importance.

2. Then, reflecting on your current work and life situation, give yourself a rating for how well you are playing out this value (1–10, with 10 meaning that you are FULLY practicing this value and highly satisfied).

TOP VALUES RATING

1. _____ . . . . _____
2. _____ . . . . _____
3. _____ . . . . _____
4. _____ . . . . _____
5. _____ . . . . _____

3. Now, take a few minutes to reflect on what you should START doing, STOP doing, and CONTINUE doing to attain full alignment with your most important values and how you spend your time.

START

STOP

CONTINUE

"*Make the difficult journey into self, being honest and candid about what motivates you and what you are truly expecting from the journey forward. Keep still and be patient for results, reminding yourself that this is not familiar territory. Listen deeply and with intention to what is coming up for you, guided by your values. Then move forward without fear, opening the doors of opportunity that are all around you. You will discover new dimensions when you explore without fear of failure, understanding that everything comes with some risk, and the greatest loss is in not trying.*"

—*Vanessa Tennyson, Executive Coach*

14

Personal Branding: Crafting Your Authentic Personal Brand

One of the most common reasons why people get a coach is to help them articulate what they stand for in a professional environment. Surprisingly, a lot of executives that are very used to talking about the purpose and positioning of their business find it challenging when they have to do that for themselves. We have heard a lot of high-powered leaders become suddenly shy or reluctant to "sell themselves," or show off.

Even though we understand the resistance, we believe that not having a clear articulation of what you stand for as a leader is a missed opportunity.

Having clarity on your personal leadership brand will help you make more meaningful connections with others by being your most authentic self, it will help you amplify your impact by focusing on what matters most to you, and it will help you pave the way to better career choices by defining what you want and what you bring as a leader.

As you prepare to help others through coaching, in this section we help you first create your own "Personal Brand Manifesto," so that you can distill your own essence and learn by doing it for the leader you know best: yourself.

Exercise: Building Your Personal Brand Manifesto

We call it a *manifesto* because it will help you translate your inner values and beliefs into a set of visible actions and choices that you want to make about how you want to show up as a leader. Write it in your own words, as the style will also reflect your essence and purpose.

This reflection will help you distill your leadership essence into a one-pager that covers five essential aspects:

I AM

Relevant aspects of your leadership journey, skills, and superpowers

I BELIEVE

Based on your values and what you believe to be true about what matters most in leadership

I ACHIEVED

Elaborate on your proudest and relevant accomplishments, ideally connected to your values

> **I WANT**
> *Based on your goals (e.g., role, organizational culture and values fit)*
> **I BRING**
> *Distill the values and skills that are most relevant to your goal*

Here's a brief example to help you visualize what the final product can look like:

I AM a people-first leader with a general manager profile that thrives in contexts of complexity, high growth, and challenge.

I BELIEVE that we do our best work when we have freedom, and we are intellectually stimulated and trusted to make the right decision regardless of hierarchy. Having grown up in a large, working-class family with many siblings, early on I learned the value of collaboration and resourcefulness. I am used to operating in chaos, and I can actually bring a steady presence to a context of disruption and uncertainty.

I ACHIEVED an unprecedented XXX% growth at job X because we had the resources, the latitude, and the support and challenge that we needed to operate as a high-performing team in a sustained way. In addition, when I led the turnaround at (company X), we were able to grow above the industry average because of the culture of empowerment and ownership that we created: even in a highly competitive environment, we were able to retain our best talent by building resilience through an authentic engagement behind our mission.

I WANT to leverage my general manager skills to build a business from the ground up, creating a culture of purposeful people that are truly empowered to achieve the unimaginable, both in the WHAT and the HOW.

I BRING 15+ years of experience in highly regulated and volatile businesses, and a resourceful mindset where I can toggle between big-picture strategy and hands-on execution. I am passionate about building teams and growing leaders that thrive in any context.

Coaching Leaders to Develop Their Personal Brand Manifesto

As you collaborate with your coachee in helping them develop their own narrative, here are some dos and don'ts to guide the process:

Do:

- Take the time to get to know them—their back story, their beliefs, and their values will be key to weave in an authentic and truly personal tone and narrative. The frameworks we have shared in prior sections can be a great foundation to this reflection.

- Help them connect their values to their achievements. When people talk first about their beliefs and values, they feel less shy about showcasing their accomplishments because they connect them to their inner compass, which we have found makes them more confident in owning their achievements.

- For what they want in the future, challenge them to be bold and make choices that represent what really matters to them. For example, if they value collaboration and they are currently in an organizational culture that drives competition and confrontation, help them articulate their desire to seek an environment more aligned with who they are and what they want.

- Encourage them to share with people they know and trust: a mentor, a close friend, or a partner can offer great insight into both substance and tone.

Don't:

- Worry about sounding "proper" or "polished." The more authentic they can be in tone and language, the more they will connect with it, making it memorable and easy to share in any environment.

- Take shortcuts. This exercise might require a couple of rounds of revisions and taking the time to let it simmer can result in a much more powerful distillation.

- Forget about connecting their achievements with the impact that was created in other people and the broader environment. When we speak about what we did and how it helped others, it creates a sense of inner confidence that usually helps people feel more confident to share with others, as it takes the focus away from "me" to "us."

"Perception is the co-pilot to reality. How people perceive you will directly impact your leadership journey, so be intentional in building your personal brand, because the biggest decisions of your career will likely be made when you are not in the room . . ."

—*Carla Harris, Wall Street Executive*

15

Redefining Impostor Syndrome

If you have been in the world of business leadership long enough, chances are that you are familiar with the concept of *impostor syndrome*, which refers to a pattern of beliefs where an individual doubts their accomplishments and has a persistent fear of being exposed as a "fraud," despite evidence of their competence. People experiencing impostor syndrome often attribute their success to luck or external factors rather than their own abilities, leading to feelings of inadequacy and a constant fear of being exposed as incompetent. The paradox is that this phenomenon is particularly common among high-achieving individuals, not only leaders but also academics, athletes, and artists, and it can significantly impact their self-esteem and mental well-being.

This is the established view of impostor syndrome, but in our work, we have come to the conclusion that instead of seeing it as a "bad thing," we can actually make friends with it and realize that it's just doing its job of protecting you by raising a flag to tell you that you are out of your comfort zone, and to be careful.

When you reframe it as a friend and not a foe, you can start channeling a lot of its latent power into positive drive. The issue with the old view of impostor syndrome is the premise that you should accept the underlying message that you are "inadequate" and intrinsically "not good enough," with the underlying assumption that this cannot be changed, which is typically associated with a fixed mindset. The new view of impostor syndrome is connected with a growth mindset: it's just telling you that you are not YET competent enough and giving you a hint that there is gold buried underneath waiting to be found.

As Adam Grant defined in his book *Hidden Potential*: "Impostor syndrome is not a clue that you're unqualified. It's a sign of hidden potential. When you think others are overestimating you, it's more likely that you're underestimating yourself."[1]

In other words, impostor syndrome is a liar, but it's a persuasive one. The key is to challenge its narrative with evidence of your accomplishments and capabilities.

When you coach people, eventually the topic of impostor syndrome will come up, and our perspective is that coaching is actually a great vehicle to turn it onto its head. When we reframe the impostor syndrome from foe to friend, what we are effectively doing is allowing it to coach us from the fearful-self into a confident and capable version of ourselves.

How do we do that? We coach our clients to go through four simple steps:

1. **Acknowledge it:** When you catch yourself doubting your abilities or your competence, instead of thinking you are sabotaging yourself, just realize that it's your friend protecting

you. Recognize and acknowledge the feelings associated with it. This involves accepting that self-doubt and insecurity are normal experiences, especially in high-achieving environments. You can even take distance from it by saying "it's just my impostor syndrome flaring up" (and not you).

2. **Listen to it:** Many of these parts of ourselves are created for the same reason: to protect us. So, when you notice the impostor syndrome, imagine you can be in dialogue with it. Just thank it for doing its job and ask it: "What are you protecting me from in this situation?" In most cases, it will be fear of failure, a sign that you are out of your comfort zone, or that this is new territory and therefore that you need to proceed with caution. Then, take the time to reflect: what exactly is making me uncomfortable? For example, it might be telling you "You are not good with numbers and this is a very analytical challenge." Even if it's not true, this is a good insight into the source of the warning and therefore pointing toward what you need to either strengthen or debunk. And often, it's the latter which takes us to the next step.

3. **Provide evidence of the contrary:** Here is where what we call "your brag catalog" will come in handy.

   Make a thorough inventory of all the major achievements you are proudest of, personally and professionally, and the skills and superpowers that you harnessed as you conquered each of them. Have this list with you at all times, nurture it and build on it as you conquer new obstacles. This will be the equivalent of a living, breathing "pep-talk in your pocket." Have the list on your phone, and make sure you keep building on it. You should even ask friends and family to contribute to it, because we often forget what we have accomplished and they will most likely sing our praises more than we do ourselves. In moments of self-doubt, go through your list, pick the skills and accomplishments that are most relevant to the situation at hand, and remind yourself of all the instances in which these superpowers served you well.

4. **Make a plan and act accordingly:** Once you have understood that the source of the discomfort is just fear of failure, that you are just out of your comfort zone in some specific areas that you now know, and that you are very capable to overcome this new challenge based on all the evidence that you have done so multiple times before, it's time to make a plan. Identify and list the challenges ahead, make a plan to overcome them leveraging your skills and knowledge, adjust accordingly and proceed with courage! In order to make your plan, check out the "Trilogy Questions" framework in Chapter 10, and have fun partnering with your new friend the impostor syndrome.

As you make friends with it, you will notice that you are actually training yourself to intentionally embrace a growth mindset. The regular practice of channeling your self-doubts into fuel for self-improvement will help you:

- **Embrace Challenges** as opportunities to learn and improve.
- **Cultivate Persistence** especially in the face of setbacks or failures.
- **Learn from Feedback** as valuable information that can help you grow and develop.
- **Adapt Strategies** to be adaptable and resourceful.
- **Celebrate Progress** regardless of the outcome.

"You're not an imposter. You're a high achiever. Those uncomfortable feelings of self-doubt are proof that you're pushing yourself to do work that matters."

—*Melody Wilding, Author*

16

The Gray Zones: Coaching, Consulting, Mentoring, and Advice

When people come to us wanting coaching, we often find ourselves needing to differentiate between Executive Coaching and other forms of support available to leaders, such as mentoring, consulting, and advising. They are all valuable and play a role in helping leaders and organizations to grow and improve, but they do it in distinct ways.

Coaching is a structured process in which the coach guides a client through a series of questions, and the client finds their own authentic answers. Good coaches avoid putting themselves at the center of the relationship by giving advice or answers, because the power lies in the client unleashing their own wisdom and resources through inquiry, active listening, feedback, and various tools to help them discover their own solutions.

Mentoring is usually a relationship between someone more experienced and someone less experienced, where the more senior person openly shares personal knowledge, experience, and wisdom, often from a similar career path. Mentoring is a relationship more than a structured process, and it can last for decades, versus coaching processes that tend to have a defined duration and structure. More often than not, mentoring is a voluntary exchange, and there is no monetary payment expected or involved.

Consulting is a profession in which an expert is engaged in helping a client (either an organization or an individual) solve complex problems and challenges for which the consultant provides specialized knowledge, analysis, and solutions. Consultancy is typically project-based and consultants conduct assessments, analyze data, and offer recommendations and implementation strategies.

Advising is typically a one-off action, and it can take place in a variety of formats: from peer advice from colleagues or friends in a specific situation, to a mentor providing perspective, or a boss recommending a course of action. As you have probably experienced first-hand, people can be quick to offer unsolicited advice with the intent of being helpful, but sometimes we could all benefit from holding back and staying curious a little bit longer. Like Michael Bungay Stanier says in his work, the "advice monster" can be quick to come up and offer opinions, but he recommends to hold back from making it your first impulse, and like a good coach, stay curious a little longer.

As a leader that will be coaching your team and colleagues, at different times you will be in a position to wear any of these four hats, and that's okay. The key is for you to have an open dialogue with your counterpart to understand what would be most helpful for them, without pushing your agenda or going with your first instinct: what works for you might not be what they want or need.

Oftentimes it's just as simple as asking: "How can I best help you?" and listen. Based on what you hear, you can clarify and establish that you can help them think through their challenge (coaching); you can offer ideas based on similar experiences you've had (mentoring); you can "solve it for them" (consulting), or you can offer concrete suggestions on a course of action (advising).

As long as you call out the nature of the support you will be providing, you can help your counterpart better understand what to expect, and it will help you frame the challenge to provide the best possible help.

Last but not least, these four options are not mutually exclusive: sometimes you can start wearing the coaching hat, openly exploring what's going on, options, and actions. Especially if you are a subject matter expert in their field, it could very well be that an option that occurred to you did not come up in their exploration, and you might feel that they could benefit from adding it to their set of alternatives. In that case, you can genuinely offer to add ideas, ideally checking first if it would be helpful for them if you share a few thoughts of your own. Most times people will welcome them, but don't be surprised or disappointed if your counterpart is so happy with the options they came up with that you hear a resounding "I am actually good with all of the options, thanks." In that case, you can rest assured that the coaching conversation brought them to a place where they are genuinely confident that the course of action is one they are committed to and excited about. And that's a great place to land!

Case Study: Navigating the Difference Between Coaching, Advising, and Mentoring

By Michael O'Reilly, Executive Coach

Background and Challenge

Sarah, a senior executive at a fast-growing tech company, had always been lauded for her intelligence and problem-solving skills. With a sharp mind and years of experience, she was often seen as the go-to person for difficult decisions and complex problem-solving within her team. In fact these skills were often identified as the driver for rapid promotions earlier in her career. However, over time, Sarah noticed a troubling pattern: her team seemed to increasingly rely on her, bringing even minor issues to her desk and waiting for her direction before taking action. This behavior led to a growing sense of frustration on Sarah's part, as she felt she was shouldering too much of the responsibility, while her team's development appeared stalled.

Upon deeper reflection and feedback from her colleagues, Sarah realized that her tendency to always provide answers had inadvertently created a dynamic where her team felt dependent on her, stifling both their and her growth. This phenomenon, known as "learned helplessness," was a direct result of her well-meaning but ultimately counterproductive application of a single over-used approach.

The Coaching Engagement

Sarah reached out for coaching to address this challenge, and her journey began with exploring the dynamics at play.

It became clear that while Sarah was a highly valued subject matter expert, her approach to leadership needed to evolve to empower her team rather than overshadow them. A significant aspect of this evolution was understanding the difference between coaching, advising, and mentoring, and how each approach could be leveraged effectively in different situations.

Coaching: Empowering Through Inquiry

Coaching, at its core, is about guiding individuals toward self-discovery and personal development. In Sarah's case, we focused on shifting her mindset from providing answers to asking powerful questions that were guided by genuine curiosity. This shift encouraged her team to think critically and take ownership of their work. For example, instead of immediately offering a solution when a team member brought a problem to her, Sarah began asking open-ended questions like, "What options have you considered?" or "How do you think we should approach this?"

This shift not only empowered her team to develop their problem-solving skills but also created a safe space where they felt valued and respected. They began to see Sarah as a leader who trusted their judgment and encouraged their growth, rather than someone who simply dictated solutions.

Mentoring: Sharing Wisdom and Experience

Mentoring involves a more personal and long-term relationship where the mentor shares their experiences and insights to guide the mentee's development. In our sessions, we

(continued)

(continued)

discussed how Sarah could balance her coaching approach with mentoring, especially when team members sought guidance on their career paths or professional growth.

Sarah started to identify moments where sharing her own experiences, both successes and failures, could provide valuable mentoring lessons for her team. By doing so, she helped them navigate challenges while still encouraging their independence. This mentoring aspect helped build deeper connections within her team, fostering trust and mutual respect.

Advising: Offering Expert Solutions

There were still instances where Sarah's expertise was necessary, and her team needed her to provide direct advice. Advising is about offering expert solutions and direction, particularly in situations that require immediate resolution or where Sarah's unique knowledge was essential.

Through our coaching engagement, Sarah increasingly recognized when her team needed her to step in with clear guidance and when it was more beneficial to adopt a coaching or mentoring approach. She also became more intentional in naming which role she was playing—whether she was coaching, mentoring, or advising—so that her team was aware of her approach and could engage accordingly.

Outcomes and Reflections

As Sarah began to implement these distinctions in her leadership style, she noticed significant changes within her team. There was a marked increase in their confidence and initiative, as they felt more empowered to make decisions and take ownership of their projects. The sense of learned helplessness that had previously permeated the team dynamics started to dissipate, replaced by a culture of collaboration and shared responsibility. She also saw her engagement scores increase, and the feedback from her team increase in richness which was an indication of the increased trust fostered within her team.

Sarah also found that by balancing coaching, mentoring, and advising, she was able to create a more dynamic and adaptive leadership style. This not only benefited her team but also alleviated her own sense of overwhelm, as she no longer felt the need to have all the answers all the time. Instead, she focused on fostering a team environment where everyone contributed to the problem-solving process.

Conclusion

This case study illustrates the importance of understanding and effectively applying the distinct approaches of coaching, mentoring, and advising in leadership. For Sarah, the journey was not just about changing her leadership style but also about redefining her role within her team. By creating a safe space for inquiry, sharing her wisdom, and providing clear guidance when necessary, Sarah was able to inspire her team to grow and thrive, while also reclaiming her own sense of balance and fulfillment as a leader.

This experience serves as a reminder that true leadership is not about being the smartest person in the room, but about empowering others to discover their own potential and capabilities.

"Everyone needs a coach. It doesn't matter whether you're a basketball player, a tennis player, a gymnast, or a leader."

—Bill Gates, Co-founder of Microsoft

17

Coaching Teams

Much of leading is around helping teams to perform at their best. In the past, that might have been through sharing experience or deciding on a structure and roles and responsibilities. However, with so much change in the air all around us, team leadership requires far more agility and adaptability than it did in the past. In other words, it requires the leader of a team to also be the team's coach.

We also know the thrill of working in a team that is creative, supportive, kind to each other, and yet helps each other to perform. We know that when trust is high, we look forward to time spent together, to solving problems and celebrating achievements together. Success not only breeds success but it is also fun—and both of these can be strong talent magnets that can make high-performing teams sustainable. Yet we also know the sense of dread when none of those things are true and teams are fraught with politics, are low in trust, and the time spent together feels like walking on eggshells or stepping through a mine field. It is the difference between these two states that makes the leadership and coaching of teams so critical.

Common Traits of High-Performing Teams

We have coached a huge number of teams over the past 20 years. It is clear to us that regardless of what the team is responsible for or the sector they operate in, there are commonalities to all high-performing teams. As a team's coach, understanding what to coach the team on is the first step, so identifying and understanding these similarities is a good place to start (see Figure 17.1).

We have observed these commonalities among high-performing teams:

- They share a clear vision of collective success.
- They actively foster trust as a performance enabler.
- They are courageous, while remaining respectful, in their debate of topics and their feedback on both what is working and what is not yet working, including about the dynamics and relationships within the team.
- They are aligned and act as one, after a robust debate, providing consistency of message and clarity of expectation to those around them.
- They fully take and accept accountability and ownership for actions that need to be implemented, for decisions, and for tasks.
- They have shared and codified behaviors that support their definition of collective success.

FIGURE 17.1 Commonalities of High-Performing Leadership Teams

Behind the high-performing team house shown in Figure 17.1 sits some critical factors that allow a high-performing team to fully engage. Having a real purpose that is preferably driving a societal benefit helps, an environment of psychological safety that allows people to feel that their views are welcomed, and a mandate for diversity and inclusion that allows them to be their authentic self are also important. In a sense these are the foundations for the house.

We also see attitudinal commonalities among high-performing teams. We know that they always rank collective success above individual success. They actively respect and value difference in all its forms. They document and hold each other to account on their shared attitudes and behaviors. They foster trust by making clear their positive intent to help each other. They have fun together—and what we mean by that is that they enjoy working together and solutioning together as much as going out together.

Coaching Your Team

Thinking about your team or the teams that you lead, how many of these points have you taken time to discuss and to codify? Can you fill in the team's definition of collective success and your attitudes and behaviors? If you talked about trust levels in your team, consistency of message to those around your team and the level of clarity they transmit, what would they say and how could these be improved? How strongly would they rate their ability to have courageous conversations and to hold each other to account? What could be done to improve these areas of high performance?

Laying Down the Foundations

We recommend that you take time, at least one and a half days, with your team to discuss these topics. It is only by doing so that the whole team will get behind the importance of these "soft" topics that are so important to their ability to deliver on the hard outcomes that will be required of them. You can use the Trilogy Questions structure to help you to find ways to improve and enhance each of these aspects of how the team operates.

In the process you will be able to gauge how strong the team's foundations are and whether or not you need to do additional work on making sure that the team environment is actually psychologically safe, inclusive, and embracing of diversity or if, in fact, you need to collectively work on these topics in the same way.

It will also help to ask your team individually and anonymously to fill out the following form so that you can calculate the average of how strongly they rank on these high-performing leadership team traits on both good and bad days:

High-Performing Team Traits	My Team Score When We're at Our Best /10	My Team Score When We're Under Pressure /10
1. We always put collective success above individual success		
2. We respect and value difference		
3. We have documented our shared values, attitudes, and behaviors		
4. We trust each other and show positive intent		
5. We regularly have courageous conversations in order to make the best decisions		
6. We give each other help-ful feedback		
7. We act as thinking partners, actively listening and feel comfortable asking for help		
8. We hold each other accountable		
9. We act as role models and pro-vide clarity to those around us		
10. We have fun together!		
Total:	/100	/100

The collated results from the table will help you and the team to see which areas you and the team rank best and worst in and therefore where the most time needs to be spent to find ways to improve.

We recommend sharing the Performance Equation, referred to earlier and slightly adapted in Figure 17.2, with teams by means of introduction and mind-setting. The team can understand the importance of spending valuable time to get these aspects of high-performing teams right and the value that this work can bring.

$$P = C \times A^2$$

Performance = Capabilities x Attitude²
—————————————————————————————
Self-Interest

FIGURE 17.2 The Performance Equation for Teams: Performance Is Equal to Capabilities × Attitude Squared, over Self-Interest

There are many other forms of mind-setting that can be helpful to apply early in a team meeting focused on success and the ways-of-working that will facilitate that success. For example, it might be useful to do your favorite get-to-know exercise or to ask the team to state what they feel most proud about. As the leader and coach, your job is to set up the team to be open to discuss what is and is not yet working and then make changes that will be helpful to everyone. Then you can help them to do the work needed to identify what those changes are and how they can be implemented.

A note of caution here. Be careful not to slip into the overuse of your leadership mantle here and be tempted to "tell them" what needs to be done differently. You are the team's coach primarily at this time, and they will never fully own what they have not co-created.

Whenever possible, it is always better to do team coaching off-site in an environment where the team is not anchored in behaving in a certain way or where they can get distracted with computers and the normal workings of an office that they are used to. It also signifies that the work the team is going to do together is important.

Determining the Team's Strategic Priorities

Once you have laid the foundations with the team, you can then move into working on the future-driven strategic house that is also common to most high-performing leadership teams.

This is where you can take the structure of the house in Figure 17.1 and insert the key strategic priorities and the relevant key performance indicators for each priority. One trap that we see many teams fall into in this process is that they overpopulate priorities such that there are so many that in fact nothing is really a priority. Any fool can make things complicated. Only geniuses can derive simplicity from complexity, so we recommend that you list no more than four strategic priorities in any given time frame. That does not mean that other activities do not need to be pursued, it is simply differentiating what the really important strategic priorities are in order to inform where resources and effort should be optimally applied.

This distillation process is never easy so this is an opportunity for you and the team's leader and coach to help differentiate between that which is critical to achieve success and that which lies more in the business as usual or nice to have categories.

Again, to help the team do this, you can use the Trilogy Questions structure to help your thinking and use a methodology that can be adopted by the whole team to solve problems in their day-to-day work together. In fact, you can use all of the techniques outlined in the previous chapters in the context of team coaching.

Consider the following example flow for how you might approach coaching your team.

Coaching Your Team: Phase 1

1. Introduction to this meeting and what the objectives are from it.

2. Mind-setting. $P=CxA2$. How high-trust environments feel versus low-trust environments.

3. Introduce your real self. Where is your happy place, and what are you most proud of that you have achieved inside or

outside of work so far. Tell us a little about how you grew up and what your values are as a result of your experiences.

4. In two groups, write a definition of collective success for this team and what it will achieve in the next two years. Then compare the outputs from each group and align on a single definition of success.

5. In two groups, suggest a maximum of four behaviors that the team wants to adopt and live by that will help them to achieve their definition of collective success.

6. Address other ways of working that will help them succeed around how they foster trust within the team, how they debate topics and then align around decisions, how they communicate with the organization beyond this team, and how they will hold themselves and each other to account.

Coaching Your Team: Phase 2

1. Thinking of the definition of collective success, what are the four most important priorities that will feed team success in the next 12 months?

2. Using Trilogy Questions, think through the What, How, Who/When of each of those four priorities.

3. Define the measures of success and the key performance indicators for each priority.

4. Design a stakeholder communication plan for the work the team has done using the Emotional Leadership structure.

We recommend that team coaching happens every three to four months to review progress, and you make any changes that are critical, although beware not to change things just for the sake of it.

Effectively, coaching your team allows you to set the culture of the team and to maintain it in a healthy and transparent manner.

"When you're surrounded by people who share a collective passion around a common purpose anything is possible."

—*Howard Schultz, Founder, Starbucks*

18

Strategic Thinking

As a leader, you have most likely applied many different approaches and frameworks of strategic thinking into your work. Now as a leader-coach, the key question for you is how you will equip others with the capabilities to think strategically.

Regardless of what models you are familiar with, the essence of strategic thinking can be distilled to a process with three core steps:

- Define your end goal, or as Stephen Covey says, "start with the end in mind."

- Explore the different paths to get to the end you have in mind, which will include understanding and analyzing your landscape, the players, and dynamics, and then assessing the different options for action.

- Build a holistic and systemic action plan to get there, including decisions for what you will and will not do, and understanding and managing the interplay of the different components of your plan.

In other words, the process of strategic thinking mirrors what we shared with you in the "Trilogy Questions" section: in Chapter 10 defining the WHAT, developing the HOW, and landing on the WHO and WHEN to bring the strategy into action in real life.

This may sound overly simple to you, but you might be surprised by how often teams are not really aligned on a shared definition of the WHAT. When we coach teams that ask us to help them with their strategic plans, we always start by conducting a round of organizational insights, and at least 50% of the time we uncover that they don't have a simple, well-defined, and aligned strategy.

Building Your Strategic House

In these instances, we roll up the sleeves and guide them through a process and framework that we call "the strategic house," as shown in Figure 18.1.

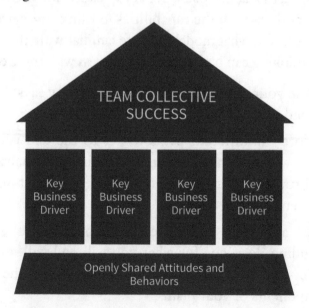

FIGURE 18.1 The Strategic House

The Roof of the House: Team Collective Success => The What

This is the purpose of the team within the business, in a way that belongs uniquely to them, defined in terms that establish concretely what success looks like.

These definitions typically include a mixture of North-Star outcomes and goals that explicitly define progress, ideally including key areas such as performance, people, and processes.

Just to give you a sense for what the output of this looks like, here's an anonymized example from the work we have done with clients, in this case with an operations team within a global CPG company:

Our purpose: We are the engine of growth that creates business value from product design to delivery.

Our goals:

- *Performance: By year X, we will increase output by X %, reduce costs by X%, and optimize our supply chain to utilize fully sustainable materials in X% of our portfolio.*

- *People: We will increase engagement by X%, focusing on people development, retention, and hiring of the top 10% talent.*

- *Processes: We will launch Project Y to streamline delivery, shortening time-to-market by X% by year XYZ.*

If these outcomes sound simple, they are by design. Good strategies need to be sharp, choiceful, and well defined. But it actually took a full day of teamwork to get to the crystallization of these definitions, which we did by asking some fundamental strategic questions, and aligning with the team on the answers and especially the choices they needed to make as a result.

To help you coach your team to outcomes of clarity and simplicity, these are some Trilogy Questions that you can leverage to help define the WHAT of this step of the strategic thinking process:

- What is going on, in a nutshell?
- What does success look like for us?
- What have we done so far?
- What is working? What is not?
- What does GOOD look like?
- What are we underestimating?
- What is a realistic view of the issue?
- What is our best thinking about this?
- What data do we have? What data do we need?
- What progress do we want to see a year from now/three years from now?
- What will be the signs that we are on track/off track?

The Pillars of the Strategic House => The How

Once your vision and goals are established, it's key to get into execution. We call this aspect of strategic thinking "pillars" because it's what holds your strategy together, giving it strength and stability.

We encourage you not to have more than four to five pillars because it will force you to make choices: in real life, companies and teams that go for a "kitchen-sink" approach of saying yes to everything end up struggling with prioritization and burnout.

We also know from experience that it's important that these pillars are not a mirror of the separate functions or roles within a team, because it will lead to siloed thinking and operating. The more cross-functional the thinking is, the better it will be for business impact and performance.

To help distinguish between what is a "pillar" and what is just an initiative or tactic, think of it in terms of its criticality to the overall success: if you remove it, would the house fall down? A good example of fairly universal pillars are areas such as "people development" or "innovation" which tend to be highly cross-functional and mission critical in most industries. If you don't have a robust strategic plan in place, you will struggle.

Aligning the Main Goals, Key Initiatives, and Capabilities

In terms of the content and essence of these pillars, the granularity and level of detail can depend on the nature of your business, but we typically focus on creating alignment, clarity, and action around three areas:

- **Main goal:** What does success look like for this strategic pillar within a defined time period, ideally with metrics?

- **Key initiatives:** What are the three to five core drivers and deliverables that will get you there, and how will you know you are on track?

- **Capabilities:** What are the mission-critical organizational capabilities that will enable your team and organization to deliver these goals and initiatives; do you have them in place or do you need to build or develop them?

To help you guide the thinking of your team to land with concrete alignment and clarity for these three areas, here are some of the Trilogy Questions that can help you. You will notice that we are going deeper, from the WHAT into the HOW and WHO/WHEN.

What

- What will success look like one year from now?
- What will be the impact on the team/the business?
- What options do we see?
- What should we START doing?
- What should we STOP doing?
- What is the level of urgency? What's driving it?

How

- What is our game plan?
- On a scale of 1–10, how realistic is this plan?
- What support/resources do we need?
- What strengths and values can we leverage?
- How will we engage our stakeholders?
- What can derail us?
- What will be the early yellow flags we will see if we are off-track?
- How will we know when we have achieved our goal?
- How will we feel when we've achieved our goal?
- How can we sustain our goal?

Who/When

- What is the first step we need to take?
- What are the following steps?
- What is the time frame for these steps?
- Who will do what by when?
- On a scale of 1–10, how committed are we?

To help you visualize the output of what good strategic pillars look like, Figure 18.2 shows an anonymized example from one of our clients, a company in the EdTech space.

Service Model	Impact & Expansion	People Development
Main goal: We define and implement scalable services for our top 50 accounts by 2025	**Main goal:** We impact student and district outcomes, effectively use data to demonstrate value and ultimately expand our products.	**Main goal:** We cultivate a fun, collaborative & inspiring environment that gets >90% engagement
Key strategies & outcomes: 1. Segmentation: define adapted service model for different products and account sizes 2. Define PM and VP roles & responsibilities to key accounts 3. Buy in from internal stakeholders with budget allocated by June 4. Launch flexible offerings that match customers' needs & schedules	**Key strategies & outcomes:** 1. We establish district goals and help districts meet them 2. XXX's are trained and prepared to lead impactful data reviews 3. We identify opportunities for additional products	**Key strategies & outcomes:** 1. We increase training sessions to 4+/year and develop tools for success 2. Launch of career plans program, including professional goals of each employee 3. We hire and scale with a DEI lens 4. Revamped PTO and family time policies 5. Relaunched innovation awards
Capabilities we have / need • Create clarity on roles and responsibilities • Communication & influencing • Courageous conversations	**Capabilities we have / need** • Change management support to customers, to help drive impact • Strategic thinking & influencing (e.g for cross-selling)	**Capabilities we have / need** • Skill development (area specific) • Managing / Leading / Coaching

FIGURE 18.2 Strategic Thinking: Building Your Pillars

The Foundation of the House => The Leadership Behaviors

As the management guru Peter Drucker said, "Culture eats strategy for breakfast." We have come across many companies and teams with flawless strategies, but if the foundation of their culture is not strong, the strategy will ultimately not fly.

This is the stage of the strategic thinking process where you will really go into leadership coaching mode, and you will create space for the team to co-create and align on a few behaviors that they need to be role models of to be able to enable the delivery of the strategy. Therefore it's important to connect the dots and create alignment between the essence of the vision and goals from the "roof," the strategic initiatives in the "pillars," and the human aspect of them as a team. So for example, if a team's collective success is to become category leaders and grow by 30% annually, and their strategies are focused on transformation and accelerated scale up, you would expect to see leadership behaviors around areas such as comfort with risk-taking and disruption, versus harmony or consensus.

When it comes to defining these leadership behaviors, there are usually two main approaches: starting from scratch or building on existing ones.

Starting from Scratch If your team is starting from scratch, there are many methodologies to develop and deploy leadership behaviors, from very simple to highly sophisticated ones that include quantitative research and validation. Since the spirit of this book is to help you build the foundations of your coaching with foundational steps first, we share a simple and effective approach that you can leverage to co-create your leadership behaviors with your team:

1. Once you finalize your strategic house (the WHAT and the HOW), ask people to step back and reflect on the nature of the work to be done to bring these initiatives to life. What capabilities and behaviors will help bring these goals and strategies to life? What strengths will you need to harness as a team to power this plan? Have them take self-reflection time to individually list no more than 10 leadership behaviors. Then, have them narrow down to their top three, and write them down on a Post-it note, one for each behavior.

2. On a large wall (or a digital board if you are working virtually), invite people to put up their top three choices. Facilitate the discussion to group them by clusters of similarity or affinity. For example, behaviors like "Collaboration" and "Teamwork" are most likely related, and you can probe to hone into the one that best reflects the collective spirit. At this stage

you will most likely start noticing patterns and shared areas, which is in itself an insightful exercise to do as a team. Group the Post-its in clusters of shared themes and give people time to reflect on which are their top choices. Give everyone three votes each to select their preferences. This can be a dynamic and fun process until you coalesce into the final three to five that have the most power and value. Channel your "coach mode" and ask powerful questions to probe and challenge the thinking, to avoid easy consensus around bland blanket behaviors like "trust," and go deeper into more specific ones like "courageous conversations" or "safe dissent." Ideally you will land on no more than three to four shared and powerful behaviors that are inspiring and aligned to the spirit of your strategic house.

3. In smaller groups, have them translate these behaviors into specific commitments, in the context of their day-to-day work, through the lens of creating specific "dos and don'ts." Make sure they reflect on their existing habits and the shifts they will need to create to live up to these behaviors. For example, if one of the chosen behaviors is to "disagree and commit" but their current tendency is to shy away from difficult conversations and postpone decisions, make sure that they state that as a shift needed when they co-create the dos and don'ts.

4. Bring it to life. Cascade it to the rest of the organization in ways that are engaging, memorable, and fun. Some of the teams that we have worked with have created company manifestos, mood videos, original songs performed by team members, and even entire leadership conferences built around these themes. Channel everyone's creative spirit, and make sure that the output speaks to all levels of the organization, from the factory floor to the CEO. We have

seen real transformations come to life and become the rallying cry of teams when they go the extra mile of translating a rather dry strategy on paper, to behaviors and commitments that ultimately become what people will remember and drive toward.

Building on Existing Behaviors   In the case of mature businesses, they are already likely to have company-wide leadership behaviors and/or values. If that's your context, it can be helpful to either validate them in light of your strategy or to create further specific meaning of the existing behaviors for your team. The good news is that you can leverage and adapt the steps outlined previously. For example, you can translate the existing behaviors into the Step 3, "dos and don'ts" for your team, your strategy, and your context.

"In the business world, the rearview mirror is always clearer than the windshield. Strategic thinking is about anticipating change and preparing for it."

—Warren Buffett, CEO of Berkshire Hathaway

19

Stakeholder Influencing

It is always easy when leading a person or a team to think that stakeholder influencing is obvious and therefore to assume that it is being done in an appropriate and optimal way. Our experience of coaching senior executives is that this is often not, in fact, the case and that it is not being thought about or pursued in all the important different ways that can help people.

As a leader who is also coaching individuals and teams, we recommend that you keep the concept of stakeholder influencing top of mind to check that the different stakeholder groups are constantly being updated and that there are clear plans to optimize stakeholder engagement.

Developing a Stakeholder Map

Drawing stakeholder maps is a very good way to keep stakeholder groups top of mind and an easy way to ensure that the different groups are being reviewed to include the ever-changing map of the comings and goings of people in organizations.

There are different types of stakeholder maps that can be drawn, or you can see if you can help teams or individuals draw a single map that is all encompassing.

For the sake of clarity, the next sections look at the different uses and groups of stakeholder maps that you might want to help people think through.

Hierarchical Stakeholders

As the name suggests, this would map those above, in differing levels of seniority, those equal to, those below, also in different levels of seniority, and those who might sit in another part of an organization horizontally or laterally that have sway on the people, decisions, or actions that a particular group or individual undertakes.

The point here is to identify and map those whose support or opposition could materially affect the implementation, reputation, or outcome of an activity. If a stakeholder can judge or opine on those things, there needs to be an actionable plan in place to make sure that they are both aware of what is going on and that they, at the very least, are not in opposition to it or the outcome.

Enterprise-wide Stakeholders

These are the people or teams across an organization who have any form of interdependency with a team or individual. These can be quite dispersed across an organization and therefore can easily be overlooked or forgotten unless properly considered and mapped.

Career Influence Stakeholders

Savvy operators are usually quite good at thinking about how to positively engage with those who can influence promotions or who can put people at risk of redundancy. However, as their leader, you need to make sure that it is not just the savvy who are doing this well. It is also important in this category to include broader networks who may be useful, not just today but also in the future.

Client and Target Client Stakeholders

This is often part of the business planning process so it is usually quite well thought out at the time of the year when budgets are prepared. However, a regular review of these allows everyone to be sure that nobody of influence or importance is being overlooked.

Partner and Supplier Stakeholders

As more and more gets outsourced to third parties, for some organizations external stakeholders can be as important to engage with as internal so mapping and planning engagement with partners and suppliers, who could be both internal and external and who may have high interdependencies, is often very important to do yet often overlooked.

Crisis Stakeholder Mapping

It is particularly helpful at the moment when a crisis is unfolding to help people to stop and think about all the stakeholders who might be affected. The pressure of a crisis moment can lead us to dive into action before taking the time to think through all those who may be touched by a crisis. Missing a stakeholder in these circumstances can have a materially negative impact on how a crisis is managed and how you navigate it in such a way as to mitigate the damage and perhaps even turn something intrinsically negative into something that can actually enhance trust.

An example of a time when this worked extremely well was the Singapore Airlines flight that was hit by extreme turbulence in 2024. The flight, originally flying from London to Singapore, was diverted to Bangkok half an hour after it hit the turbulence. One person died as a consequence and many others were hospitalized following the incident. Singapore Airlines immediately set about a comprehensive stakeholder engagement plan, not just for the passengers who were affected by what had happened but across all the other stakeholder groups that they had mapped. This included the families of all the passengers, setting up Facebook and Instagram feeds that were updated several times an hour to provide information to anyone who might have wanted it, regular press updates, laying on an emergency evacuation flight to take passengers who could fly on to Singapore and making and tracking hotel reservations for those in transit in Singapore. They even announced changes in service policy to passengers and all crew immediately following the incident to prove that the lessons learned had immediately been acted upon.

So good and comprehensive was their response that one PR magazine's lead article was headlined: *"A Singapore Airlines Passenger Died on a Flight Because of Extreme Turbulence. The Company's Response Is a Master Class In Emotional Intelligence"*. In an industry known for PR disasters, Singapore Airlines' response to the tragedy is a template for handling a crisis well. Much, it is fair to say, because they had their stakeholder map fully populated, and each section had its own distinct plan.

Life Stakeholders

Of course, it is also worth thinking about those beyond work that matter to an individual. It always surprises us when we are helping senior executives build stakeholder maps how many people can get overlooked until we consistently ask, "Who else should be on this map and is currently missing?"

We also find it useful as we build the maps to think about the current status of the relationship with someone on a particular map compared to the desired relationship, visibility, or level of support wanted and needed from that person. This draws into focus the people who need more work to engage positively with.

Many organizations today are also highly matrixed and the more matrixed an organization is the more complex the stakeholder map tends to be. So having something written down that is easy to review allows them to keep top of mind all of the stakeholders, regardless of the complexity of the map.

Looking Forward

Once we have helped people think through their stakeholders, we then need to help them draw up the actual engagement plans that will keep stakeholders on their side and supportive. These plans might include anticipating touchpoints that provide engagement opportunities and the creation of communication points that would help as well as the informal moments that allow someone to gain support or positive influence.

For those wishing to Lead with Coaching, taking the time to coach and drill down on their stakeholder mapping and engagement planning will be time well spent. It also helps you as the leader understand your own stakeholder maps and build your own comprehensive engagement plan.

"People do not buy goods and services. They buy relations, stories, and magic. Stakeholder influence is about creating value in relationships, not just transactions."

—Seth Godin, *Author*

20

The Power of Safe Feedback

As leaders and coaches it is often easy to categorize people's traits into strengths and weaknesses. Many believe that coaching someone on how to overcome their weaknesses is the best value add to that person. Yet this traditional way of thinking about how to help someone is, in our view, deeply flawed and overly simplistic. It might have been born from the early days of how to give feedback in which it was commonly accepted that feedback took the form of a sandwich. The bread served as an acknowledgment of someone's good points and the filling, generally somewhat thinner than the bread, served as the part they could most usefully work on. Perhaps you do not need us to remind you what this sandwich became colloquially known as! Thankfully, today, feedback structures tend to be more sophisticated and often work on the principle of identifying a person's key strengths and then looking at what happens if they are either underused or overused.

This really came home to us when listening to the coach of the Dutch female hockey team one year when they won an Olympic gold medal. The team's coach described how he had worked with the team for four years in the run up to the games and how he had identified one player as being particularly talented. He saw that she would be a tremendous asset to the team with the potential to score goals with the most incredible forehand. However, he identified that her backhand was nowhere near as strong, so for the first three years he was coaching her, he worked with her all the time on how to improve her backhand. Over time, it improved, but only very marginally. Worryingly, over the same period of time, her forehand superpower declined gradually. A year before the Olympics, her coach abandoned any attempt to improve her backhand, solely focusing on bringing back and improving to the full extent her incredible forehand. She went on to score four goals in the most important game, helping the team to win the gold medal. We think for all those Leading with Coaching, this is a good lesson to learn vicariously.

A good place to start when coaching someone you lead is to identify their strengths and help them to accelerate, accentuate, and amplify them so that they can be used to their full potential. This also helps build confidence while at the same time helping a person acknowledge that there is such a thing as a strength overplayed, and that when that happens it can become less helpful than when applied appropriately.

By example, many senior leaders we coach have optimism as a trait—often in abundance. It is an extremely useful trait to have as a leader as it is infectious and so allows those being led to believe that the difficult is attainable. It helps leaders get through very difficult times, and it helps leaders to find answers to intricate problems as their brains are hardwired to believe that there is a solution to everything. The issue arises when the strength of optimism is overused. It can be perceived as blind optimism. Others may come to see this leader as detached from reality, overly ebullient, or come to mistrust forecasts or budgets that are consistently proven to be overly optimistic or unrealistic. And thus a very useful strength, when overused, can become a real hindrance. So, the art of coaching the optimistic leader is to make sure that the trait is used in its most positive way and not overused to the degree that it becomes unhelpful to either the leader or those around the leader.

Courageous Conversations

We are all told from the start of our careers that feedback is extremely helpful and that we should embrace it. Unfortunately, that is not often how receiving feedback can feel. It can feel like pure, unadulterated criticism. It can feel like a personal attack to the benefit solely of the person proffering it. It can feel unfair that we have been misunderstood either from the perspective of our intent or from what we actually did. It can also feel like the context of the environment can be ignored.

Many of the negative feelings we can get from being offered feedback are because we sense that the person offering it to us has an ulterior motive in doing so that is more in their own interests than in ours. We all have amazing "bullshit" monitors that detect if someone is lying or if someone's intent is other than what they say it is.

We were also taught early in our careers that the best way to give feedback is to do it in the form of a sandwich, the top and bottom slices being the positive feedback and the filling in the middle being the stuff we are supposed to take on board and address. The issue with this structure is that we all know it so we ignore the bread and just focus on the filling. We tune out anything positive the person has to say in anticipation of the negative.

When we couple the sandwich with the question of someone's intent, it is hardly surprising that feedback can often be more of an assault than a learning opportunity.

As the coach of your people, you need to be skilled at offering feedback in such a way that makes the learning easily accessible.

Check Your Intent

The first step in providing good feedback that actually helps someone learn, understand their impact in a way they were previously blind to, or gain awareness that has been illusive is for you as their leader and coach to be entirely clear of your intent: The intent to help them.

Before offering someone feedback, really investigate whether your intent is to help, enable, and open them up to possibility. If you are in any doubt about your intent, wait until you can be entirely certain of your positive intent toward the person you are offering feedback to. See Figure 20.1.

Criticism **Intended to hurt?**
Criticism is an opportunity to tell someone something you don't like about them or what they're doing.

Feedback **Intended to help?**
Feedback is an opportunity to ask a person if they would like to hear something that may help them.

FIGURE 20.1 A Reminder to Check Intention Before Offering Feedback

This also applies to extreme situations when you might be angry, surprised, or shocked. Knee jerk feedback is rarely taken well.

Once you are clear as to your intent, you can then think of offering feedback, or, as we like to call it, having a courageous conversation.

One-to-One Courageous Conversations

The traditional sandwich structure tends not to have the best results, so we suggest that as someone's leader and coach that you take a more thoughtful and thorough approach to offering feedback.

1. Start by telling someone what you think, authentically, they are really good at. Give examples and offer praise for the times when they have brought about demonstrably positive results. Ask them for their reaction to what you have said to them about what you think that they are really good at.

2. Move onto what you think that they would benefit from by doing more of. This could be accentuating or amplifying behaviors or improving their capabilities.

3. Move onto what you think that they would benefit from by doing less of.

4. Finally, think of anything that they should start doing that they are not doing at all that would be to the benefit of themselves or others and what they should stop doing that is unhelpful to themselves or others.

You end up with a clear and balanced structure:

Good

More of

Less of

Start

Stop

The advantages of this structure are many. Often feedback is nuanced and can vary depending on whether it is based on strengths being under or overused. It can also depend on whether someone is simply having a good day or a bad day, or whether they are under pressure or stressed. By using the structure, you allow for these contexts and for the fact that feedback is almost always inherently contradictory depending on circumstances. It also avoids the sole focus on what someone needs to address or improve by addressing those in a more rounded and subtle way.

Courageous Conversations in Team Settings

Given the fact that most teams are time poor and do not spend enough face-to-face time together, it is often a good idea in team meetings to allow the space for courageous conversations. However, as the team coach and leader, you will want to make sure that these conversations are impactful and safe to have.

To do this, we suggest that you give the teams unfinished sentences to facilitate their individual one-to-one conversations.

Examples of the unfinished sentences you could provide to them would be the following structure:

- Something I really respect about you is. . . . . . .
- Something I think that you could change that would help you is. . . . . . .
- Something you could change that would help me is. . . . . . .

In a team setting, each person would have the opportunity to speak to each member of the team one-to-one to address the unfinished sentences. Surprisingly, these one-to-one conversations can be done quickly while remaining extremely useful and impactful. We would suggest between three and five minutes for each person in the pair.

In conclusion, giving feedback opportunities the proper structure that keeps it safe, digestible, and yet honest and helpful is a skill that can only benefit leaders, individuals, and teams.

"Feedback is the breakfast of champions."

—*Ken Blanchard, Author*

21

Coaching for Empowerment

When people think of empowerment, they often associate it with delegation. But in fact, empowerment is much more than just that. Delegation is to entrust a task or responsibility to another person, typically one who is less senior than oneself, whereas empowerment is to give someone the authority or power, making them stronger, more confident, and feeling more in control of what they need to deliver. In the context of business, empowerment ultimately means that people are authorized and enabled to do what the business needs. To unlock your organization's ability to perform at the highest standard and to energize your people, you need to capture a greater sense of empowerment and ownership.

Practicing Empowerment

In real life, what we see is that everyone wants to give and receive more empowerment, but often leaders and teams get stuck in how to effectively put it into practice.

Here are a few fundamentals to increase your confidence and ability to empower more, empower better, and empower faster.

Empowerment Is Not a One Size Fits All Approach

Let's face it, you would not give the same level of autonomy or power to a person in their first month on the job, as you would give to someone seasoned who knows the ins and outs of the company.

Good leaders know how to do gradual empowerment, adapting the ask and the task to the person and the context, based on their skill and will. For less experienced team members (low skill), empowerment should begin with clear guidance and structured support. As they gain in competence, you can gradually increase their autonomy by assigning more complex tasks and decision-making responsibilities, always ensuring they have the necessary resources and mentorship to succeed. For those at higher levels of seniority or expertise, empowerment involves providing them with strategic responsibilities and the freedom to lead initiatives, while still offering occasional feedback and opportunities for professional growth.

As a leader-coach, you can adapt your coaching style when you empower, based on where people are on the Empowerment Readiness Matrix, shown in Figure 21.1.

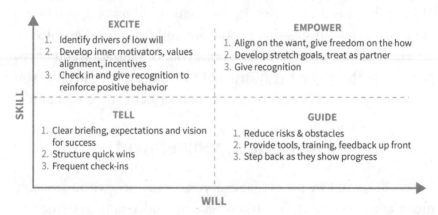

FIGURE 21.1 The Empowerment Readiness Matrix

The position of your team members in this matrix can be dynamic, as different people will have varying levels of skill and will be based on the situation, the context, and their own strengths.

Someone could be very high skill and will in project management, but they could be low skill and will in stakeholder influencing, so you have to adapt your choices to the situation.

Structuring an Empowerment Conversation

Once you have established where they are and how you will guide them, as a leader-coach it is key to have a structured and consistent approach to what we believe is an underutilized asset: a well-structured empowerment conversation.

Figure 21.2 shows a coaching framework that we have used effectively with leaders at all levels, and we guide you step by step to leverage its power.

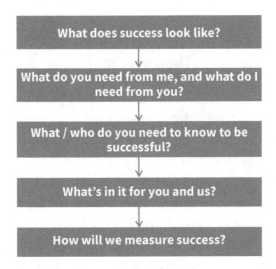

FIGURE 21.2 The Empowerment Framework

Step 1: Define the WHAT; What Does Success Look Like?

This sets the expectations and standards that you want to establish, to make sure that you see eye to eye with your team, especially when it comes to having a shared definition of what good looks like. This is a common pitfall we see with our clients, where the leader does not take the time to give concrete references of the standard that is expected, and then if delivery falls short, it creates frustrations and speedbumps that could have been prevented just by making sure that your vision is calibrated to the same criteria.

In order to coach your team in this step, you can prompt with questions such as:

- What does GOOD look like?
- How can I set you up for success?
- What is the kind of progress/impact we want to create: progressive, incremental, transformational?

Step 2: What Do You Need from Me, and What Do I Need from You?

This creates a healthy balance of interdependence for independence. By setting the scene for how you will operate together, you are actually defining where you are passing on the baton so that the person can run and act autonomously, giving them greater agility and room to maneuver. This helps people gain confidence, broaden their perspectives, and develop a more robust sense of autonomy. This process enables individuals to become independent not just by their own efforts, but through the collective support and shared knowledge of their community or team, leading to more sustainable and effective independence.

At this stage, you can leverage coaching prompts including:

- What behaviors, capabilities, and mindset do you need to achieve?
- What resources do you need? How can I help you get them?
- What do you need from me?
- At what points in the process do you need me? How will I know?

Step 3: What and Who Do You Need to Know to Be Successful?

This helps to be aligned regarding the context and key stakeholders. Leaders often forget that a key asset and edge they can have over some of their team members is their organizational knowledge of who is who, and how things get done, formally and informally. Opening these doors and unpacking the latent ramifications of an action within the organization will help your team anticipate needs and implications, liaise with the right counterparts, and understand how the dots connect between their actions and the bigger picture.

These are some helpful prompts to coach them to go deeper in this step:

- What is the business context for this?
- On a scale of 1–10, how comfortable are you navigating this context?
- What do you know, and don't know that I can help with?
- What is missing?
- What is the impact of these actions/your plan in the broader context of the business?
- Who are your key stakeholders?

- What do you need from them, and what do they need from you?
- What level of trust do you feel you have with them? If not high enough, what can you/we do to increase their trust and set you up for success?

Step 4: What's in it for You and Us?

At this stage, the conversation will help you make sure that you are creating a real sense of ownership, purpose, and intrinsic motivation. In the spirit of focusing their time on what matters most, leaders sometimes need to delegate lower-value tasks, and if people are not motivated or do not feel true ownership, they will often stall or have a half-hearted commitment. At this stage you want to make sure that they see and understand the value of the work they will do, how it will benefit them professionally and sometimes even personally, but also how it can positively impact the organization at large. In this step you should also identify any unexpected risks and consequences, to help them get ahead of it and increase their comfort level with their ability to manage and lower these risks.

To help make sure that people are on board, motivated, and set up for success, you can align on:

- How does this fit in the big scheme of things: how will it help us achieve our overarching goals?
- How will it help YOU achieve your goals?
- On a scale of 1–10, how motivated are you?
- What is missing?
- What is the impact of not achieving it?
- What will be the consequences?
- What can you do to manage risk? On a scale of 1–10, how comfortable are you navigating this context?

Step 5: How Will We Measure Success?

This is a crucial landing point to make sure that your expectations are aligned, and that you are creating true accountability and foresight of early yellow flags, so that they raise them when they need you, and before it's too late. This is not only a key moment of the conversation for empowerment, it also increases everyone's comfort level with the unexpected things that can go wrong, so that off-track does not become a derail.

To help make sure that people are on board, motivated, and set up for success, you can align on:

- How will we know we are on track?
- How will we know we are OFF track?
- What will be the early signs?
- What is your contingency plan?
- When do you need my involvement?
- How often do we want to check in?

Looking Forward

In conclusion, empowerment is vital in a leader-coach role, and a good conversation is the cornerstone of this process. By engaging in meaningful dialogues, you can tap into your team members' aspirations, challenges, and ideas, creating an environment where they feel valued, heard, and trusted. These conversations are opportunities for leaders to delegate authority and power (not only tasks), to set clear expectations, and provide the encouragement needed for team members to take true ownership of the work. Through open and supportive communication, leaders can instill confidence, foster autonomy, and motivate their team to take on greater responsibilities. Ultimately, a strong conversation is not just about giving directions, but about empowering others to think critically, act independently, and contribute to the team's success in meaningful ways.

To sum this up, Figure 21.3 leaves you with this visual reminder of the five coaching steps to a productive empowerment conversation, and the benefits it will create.

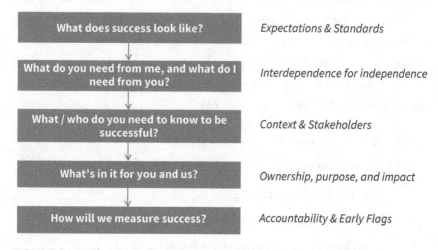

FIGURE 21.3 The Benefits of Empowerment at Every Step

"If you look after your staff, they'll look after your customers. It's that simple. Empowerment comes from trust and the freedom to do what's best."

—*Richard Branson, Founder of Virgin Group*

22

Great Team Meetings in Any Environment

Let's face it, even though technology has transformed our lives and the way we work, there are still a few significant interactions in which a meeting remains the preferred way to get things done. Business meetings are crucial for decision-making, problem-solving, and team building within an organization.

As a coach-leader, you can now take these meetings to the next level by infusing some best practices that can help you go from "getting things done" to truly building engagement, alignment, and momentum. Infusing coaching into your team meetings can improve communication, accountability, and team dynamics.

Here are a few best practices that can help you create an edge to your meetings:

- **Be prepared:** Define the purpose, agenda, objectives, and desired outcomes in both business and leadership terms.

For example, *'we want to align on roles and responsibilities for project X, and we want to define the mindset and behaviors that we will need as leaders for this project'*.

- **Invite the right people:** Look beyond functional expertise, making sure you have a diversity of thinking and management styles to enrich collaboration, and pressure-test ideas and solutions through different angles.

- **Focus on co-creation, discussions, decisions, and problem-solving:** Information sharing is a poor use of everyone's time when you can send pre-reads and make sure people are up to speed by sharing documents or reports to review ahead of time. This gives participants a chance to prepare and be ready for the highest added value aspects of collaboration.

- **Take the time to check in and set the tone:** Use simple prompts to kick things off and establish the mindset for how people want to show up. You can leverage traffic light color coding, one-word intents, or prompts such as "what do you bring with you, what do you need to leave behind?" to create a transition between what took place before, and how they want to show up in this new context.

- **Make sure the WHAT is clear:** If you sense people are going in circles or getting tripped up, it's often because they are not (yet) aligned on the WHAT and therefore they are likely to be struggling with the HOW. Go back to the principles in the Trilogy Questions to create clarity and alignment.

- **Give a voice to everyone:** In most teams it is common to see dynamics with some members being more vocal, and others who are quieter. Actively involve all participants, asking for their input and soliciting their views. For those who need time to process, it's okay to give them a heads up that you will ask everyone for their views, so that they don't feel they are put on the spot if they are not ready.

- **Practice C.A.L.M. active listening:** Leveraging the techniques we shared in the previous chapters, play back people's views and build on them as needed, acknowledging their contributions and addressing any questions or concerns.

- **Empower your team by having them summarize actions and next steps:** It's very tempting for team leaders to want to have the "final word" and in the spirit of saving time, the most senior leader tends to wrap up a meeting by listing the actions, next steps, and owners. This is a missed opportunity to actually give the power to your people by having them summarize agreements, actions, and next steps. This small shift in how you conduct meetings will create a much greater sense of psychological ownership. By simply asking "What have we agreed on?" and letting your team own the wrap up, you are "passing the baton" and taking empowerment to the next level.

- **Gather live feedback:** Plan for meeting timings by regularly allocating a few minutes at the end to reflect on what worked well, and what you can do better next time. This will create a culture of ongoing improvement and openness to feedback that will help get sharper at both the WHAT and the HOW of your ways of working as a team.

- **Follow through:** Make sure that there are good summary and meeting notes available to all participants by either rotating this task, or even assigning it to the multiple AI companions that are readily available in virtual or hybrid environments such as Zoom and Microsoft Teams, that are able to take notes, tag owners, and follow up if you prompt them to.

Implementing these best practices will help ensure your meetings are productive, efficient, and valuable for all participants.

"If you can't feed a team with two pizzas, your meeting is too large. Meetings should be small enough to be productive, focused on decisions, not on endless discussions."

—*Jeff Bezos, Founder of Amazon*

23

When to Get the Pros In: Hiring External Executive Coaches

Our hypothesis throughout this work has been that it is a prerequisite for leaders today to incorporate coaching competencies at the center of their leadership skill set and leadership style. While we believe this to be both true and necessary, we also know that there is a time and a place to bring in the professionals and hire external Executive Coaches.

We do not intend to be prescriptive as to each and every circumstance in which a leader, a leadership team, or a company might want to move from the do-it-yourself model to one that relies on external expertise; rather, we offer some examples of when it can be helpful to consider it.

External 1:1 Executive Coaching: To Have or Not to Have

The challenge with senior people being coached by internal coaches is often that much of what a senior leader is contending with is either confidential, highly personal, has impact on colleagues, or requires the type of objective thinking partnership that transcends personal agendas or interests. In other words, it requires the coach to be agnostic in terms of their own interests and agenda, entirely objective in their thinking and questioning, and able to independently help someone through the three lenses of the person, their role, and the organization in which they work. An external coach has an obligation to provide value in each of these spheres. So as a rule of thumb, we recommend that if you are a leader operating in the top 5–10% of the entire leadership population of your organization you should think about engaging a professional, external, Executive Coach.

Generally, Executive Coaching relationships with external coaches are time bound. Yet it is not uncommon for a senior leader to engage with the same coach at different junctions throughout their careers. For example, at moments of promotion, a big expansion of role responsibility, or when dealing with a new or extended set of stakeholders; broadly at significant times of transition.

The advantage of working with the same coach at different career stages is that you do not need to rebuild the trust or the history anew each time you want to engage with an external Executive Coach, which makes the process faster and more efficient. Further, working with the same coach normally means that the coach has the overall context around the person they are coaching and the organization, or type of organization, in which they work.

It is also possible that a senior leader may simultaneously engage with an internal coach, an external coach, and an internal or external mentor. In our experience, as the complexities of leading people and organizations increase almost daily, the leaders who are most open to seek out and accept help, who challenge, support, and value difference of thinking are the most likely to succeed over the long term.

The advantage of this is that the time spent with these supporters is time to reflect, to pause, and to think things through, which many leaders find is not easy to do when actively engaged in their day-to-day work. It is also a way of keeping their own coaching skills and coaching menu up to date as they experience what it feels like to be coached. More and more, Executive Coaches are also able to provide some of the insights that used to be provided by management consultants in the sense that most of us work in multiple sectors and in many different types of organizations which allows us to provide insights as to how other leaders are tackling some of their challenges. It is a way of bringing the outside in which is a perspective that internal coaches rarely have.

So overall, our recommendation is for leaders to consider engaging with an external Executive Coach as they near the top leadership levels in their organization. We have also seen in recent years much more acceptance and appreciation for the need, use, and cost of external coaches by organizations that recognize the value-add that they provide, that wish to show support and give recognition to their senior leaders, and that wish to engage in their continual development to ensure the strongest possible talent bench and succession options for their most senior people. In the scale of things, the investment required to hire an external Executive Coach is marginal at most if it helps them to perform better, learn and develop as leaders, and increases their adaptability and job satisfaction.

Almost all global organizations recognize this to be the case and are becoming much more sophisticated in their approach, selection, use, and deployment of external Executive Coaches.

External Team Coaching: To Do or Not to Do

The challenge for most leaders who double as the team leader and the team coach is to decide when they are in which role, how to flex between each of those roles, and how to be an independent observer able to facilitate the team's thinking as the team coach versus be invested, participatory, and able to give direction and set clear expectation as the team leader. The juxtaposition of these two roles gets more difficult the more senior the leadership team you are working with.

Another obvious factor is the team dynamic, how high or low trust levels are and how advanced a team is in terms of its articulation of collective success. Teams with a well-established and healthy culture, defined ways of working, and a clear operating cadence are quicker to accept the leader as their coach than those who are at an earlier stage of development as a team.

Often newly established, relatively senior teams benefit the most from having an external team coach. This also allows for the leader to fully participate in the team coaching with far less risk of the conflict inherent between trying to deliver on both roles simultaneously. It also allows for the leader to be more present and a better observer of the team and its individual members which, especially when constructing a new team, can be extremely valuable to a leader.

However, if any leader is finding it a challenge, or being told by a team that there is a challenge, around being both the leader and the team's coach, then it is better to engage external coaches.

Many organizations are starting to use team coaching more now than ever before. Some sectors, such as fast-moving consumer goods companies, have much higher adoption and experience in their use of it than, for example, the financial services sector. However, we are seeing much more interest across the board in team coaching delivered by external coaches as organizations better appreciate the return on investment from it. When delivered to a team of between 8 and 10 people, the cost per head is low and, if well delivered, the impact high.

Increasingly, team coaching is also a great way to pulse-check an organization and the quality of leadership that different functions at different levels are experiencing from the relevant leaders on the team. Team coaching can be coupled with organizational insights reviews, where a coach speaks to a broad range of people in an organization to ascertain how well, for example, the vision or strategy is understood and being implemented and what additional information or help they would like to enhance their impact. So increasingly, team coaching has a broader and deeper application and reach beyond just the team being coached, further increasing its effectiveness.

Generally, for senior or newly constituted teams it is well worth exploring external team coaches that can then be paired with the leaders adopting a coaching leadership style day-to-day.

Keep It in the Family: Ultra High Net Worth Family Coaching

The one time we would suggest only considering the use of an external Executive Coach is for the purpose of coaching Ultra High Net Worth (UHNW) families and within their operating businesses.

The dynamics of families working together or supervising professional managers in family owned businesses requires an even greater level of objectivity and independence. This does not mean that even family members who are leaders within a family business cannot lead with a coaching style; they can and should. However, for the purposes of 1:1 coaching or team coaching, the level of involvement, intrinsic interest in success and strategy, and a natural challenge around objectivity means that an external coach is far better suited to navigate the systemic challenges of family owned businesses or family dynamics around wealth preservation, custodianship, and growth.

It is very often good idea in family owned businesses to invest in the creation of a coaching culture as it provides a balance of power between family members and those who work with and for them.

This type of coaching is quite specialized so it is important when looking for a coach for this type of work that you find a firm or a person who has the correct experience in this niche field.

Best Practices for Finding the Right Coaching Firm and the Right Coach

If you do decide to investigate the use of external Executive Coaches, it is important to understand the type of coaching firm and the type of coach you might be looking for.

The first question is whether or not a particular firm has the credentials necessary to be credible and impactful with you and your people. They should be able to be clear about how their coaches are trained and qualified, be clear as to where their experience and expertise lies, and the type of work they are best suited to do. It is important to understand, for example, whether their coaches have a business and leadership background, a psychological or organizational development background, or whether they have drawn on other experiences to develop their coaching practice and expertise.

One of the issues with the world of executive coaching today is the plethora of coaches out there and their varied experience, training, and areas of focus. It is also important, especially for international organizations wishing to deploy coaching across geographies, to understand the cultural awareness and experience of firms and coaches.

Increasingly, the world of executive coaching is divided between the top echelon firms that generally have experienced business professionals and leaders who have then requalified, normally with an academic qualification, and the more mid-market firms. The former tend to have a strong cadre of coaches who are hand-picked and supervised and developed by the firm they work with. The latter often act as coaching consolidators who vet coaches but are not responsible for any uniformity of approach or quality across the coaches they represent. Further, as more digital coaching offerings become available, the democratization and commoditization of coaching is an advantage in that it becomes more broadly available and accessible yet has the potential disadvantage of not being of consistent quality or methodology and therefore risks achieving varied outcomes.

NOTE: The basic point is that good research into the type of coaching firm and the type of coach you would want to work with is important in choosing a supplier. Very often, word of mouth and advocacy by people who have used a particular firm or coach is a good way of narrowing down the field as it can be wide and densely populated. A strong recommendation from someone you trust will save you time and energy and often ensure the best use of your time and investment.

Many buyers of coaching assume that it is desirable for a coach to have had directly relevant experience—a lawyer who is coached by a coach who has been a lawyer, for example. We challenge this approach. What is important is that a coach has the context and experience of coaching in the field but often being too closely associated with a particular set of experiences or a particular profession can result in the relationship being more akin to mentoring than to coaching, which are actually distinct activities and disciplines. We argue that business acumen and experience coupled with leadership familiarity and a broad understanding of the context of a particular sector or profession are of greater value than a "I've done exactly your job" approach.

We believe that it is also important for coaching firms to represent as much diversity as possible in such a way that mirrors the existing or desired level of diversity in an organization. This might be diversity of experience, cultures, operating environments and geographies, backgrounds, sectors, gender, and all the many other facets of diversity. Yet within that level of diversity a commonality of approach or framework will ensure that there is a consistency of outcome that ensures that the desired return on investment from coaching is achieved, no matter where the coaching is taking place or delivered.

We would also add that firms and coaches would normally be open to taking the time to get to know the client, be that in the form of the company or the leader or team. They should demonstrate commercial and personal curiosity as to what good looks like, be interested in an organization's current and desired culture, and what is working or not working yet for a particular leader or leadership challenge. This process, which is normally free as part of the relationship building process, allows you to check that you feel the fit is right and the type of questioning and dialogue is of the quality that you would expect.

Choosing a coaching provider is often a major decision and one that can have long lasting benefit—choose wisely.

Making the Most of the Pros

Once you have selected a coaching firm as your provider or some possible coaches as options able to meet your coaching objectives, you are then able to be deliberate about making the final decision—which coach to select.

Chemistry Is Key

The first phase of this would be to do a one-hour meeting with each of your chosen coaches to establish how comfortable you will feel to work with that person. We call these meetings chemistry meetings as that is exactly what they are designed to establish. These meetings will usually include an exploration of your coaching objectives, perhaps a look at career ambitions and aspirations and what would need to happen for those to be achieved, a look at your stakeholder constellation and which of those relationships might need work, and perhaps a look at how the coaching relationship might work in terms of frequency, location, and how to get a briefing from your line manager.

Terms of Engagement

Once you have chosen the coach you think best suited to you and your objectives, then you should move into agreeing on the number of hours to be delivered, the cost, the inclusion of a feedback gathering process, and any process requirements from the sponsor of the coaching. These might include reporting procedures, invoicing, organizational briefings, and so forth. You might also cover the use of any psychometric tools or other interventions that could form part of the coaching process.

Feedback and Insights

Our strong recommendation is that all 1:1 coaching assignments should include a feedback and insights process. This would be done by the coach actually speaking with 8–10 key stakeholders to understand what the person is good at, could do more of, less of, start, or stop. This would be done in addition to any on-line type of 360-degree feedback that might be done as part of the general human resources approach to feedback. This is really important as this provides the coach the independent data on how others experience the person being coached. Without it, the world will only ever be seen as described by the person being coached. This has the potential to obscure critical information from both the coach and the person being coached that, were it visible and known, could really help address blind spots or the impact that a leader actually has as opposed to the leadership impact they intend to have or need to have.

This is also an integral part of team coaching whereby the coach speaks to each member of the team to investigate what is working within the team, what is not yet working, what the key objectives would be for the team from the team coaching, and so on.

Clarify Personal and Organizational Objectives

Marrying the objectives of the person being coached and those of the organization from the coaching to be done is a critical first step in building an effective coaching relationship that has impact where it is most needed and most expected. This is usually done in the first session, followed by the beginning of the feedback and insights process and knowing the areas to be most deeply investigated in alignment with the objectives.

A^2 Attitude Squared: It Makes All the Difference

The impact and effectiveness of any coaching assignment depends very much on the attitude and engagement of the person being coached. The process works best when meetings are held with sufficient frequency, optimally about once per month for two hours each session. It is also incumbent on the person being coached to actively participate in the process, do the work that it will require, be open to the learnings available, and to embrace the experience so that they derive the very best value from it.

Not making the coaching sessions a time priority, expecting the coach to prove the value without actively and enthusiastically engaging in the process, will significantly reduce the power and impact that a coaching relationship can have. So, we urge those lucky enough to have access to an external Executive Coach to value the badge of honor, talent recognition, and privileged development opportunity that it is.

Virtual or In Person?

In some ways the learnings from the COVID-19 pandemic have been extremely helpful. Coaching went from an almost always in-person process to an almost entirely virtual interaction. Now that we are free of any restrictions, we are able to take the best of both worlds.

While at the most senior levels, there can be no doubt that coaching in person is the best option, combining in-person sessions with virtual sessions allows for a level of easy access and efficiency that ensures that the coaching interactions can be consistently timed and paced which is a prerequisite for coaching to work. It means that even when travel schedules are tight or time spent on travel is inefficient, the coaching relationship can continue.

In our experience, for 1:1 coaching, using a combination of face-to-face time and virtual access makes the most sense and optimizes the coaching relationship. Virtual coaching sessions tend to be between one and two hours in length whereas, depending on the agenda of each session, in-person meetings tend to be between two and three hours each.

For team coaching, while some benefit can be derived from virtual meetings, we strongly recommend in-person meetings for the creation of high-performing teams.

Number of Coaching Hours per Assignment

The number of hours per assignment is highly variable depending on the expected outcomes from the coaching, the complexity of the coachee's operating environment, their seniority, the level of change, either operational change or behavioral change, that needs to be navigated, and a host of other factors.

However, any change will only be embedded as a result of consistency and frequency so usually this requires a minimum of 12 hours of coaching, which can stretch up to 18 hours (excluding stakeholder interaction and feedback and insights processes) for the more challenging coaching requirements.

Less senior leaders can also benefit from shorter coaching journeys if the coaching output is clearly defined and of a reasonable scope. Although even in these circumstances, we do not recommend fewer than four sessions of a minimum of 1.5 hours each.

Coaching can also be used to mediate relationships and these interventions can be shorter and better defined depending on the issues at hand and the severity of the relationship breakdown.

So in essence, the number of hours required per assignment is dependent on the coaching brief and expected outcomes.

Most coaching companies and good coaches try to limit the number of times that coaching assignments get extended. This is to ensure that the relationship does not develop into one of dependency and to ensure that they do not become overly familiar and thereby less challenging and creative in thought and discussion.

"The best coaches know your strengths and push you further, but they also know when to pull you back to refine and ground yourself."

—*Marc Benioff, CEO of Salesforce*

24

Want to Build a Coaching Culture?

Building a coaching culture is an organizational development intervention that is, by nature, also a systemic intervention. Creating a coaching culture within an organization is essential for fostering business growth, continuous learning, and innovation. By embedding coaching into the fabric of the company, leaders can take ownership of their development, enhancing their skills, confidence, and overall performance.

Preparation

One of the challenges around the ambition to build a coaching culture is to be clear as to the purpose and outcome required from such an investment.

Success can be defined in multiple ways—to increase speed and agility at all levels of an organization, to improve the quality of thinking around problem-solving and creativity, to enhance empowerment and the ability of people to work better with each other and in teams, to encourage the inclusion of a broader base of idea contribution, or to provide better early warning systems of things that are either going well or going wrong. It is also possible to want all of the aforementioned and more as outcomes from building a successful coaching culture.

A well-implemented program will also facilitate the ability to have regular meaningful performance and development discussions and better succession insight and planning.

Picking a few focus points that perhaps are not yet fully formed ways of working that would greatly improve the performance and happiness of an organization is an important place to start.

Ultimately, a coaching culture should improve the performance of an organization, make it a better and more enjoyable place to work, improve decision-making, business planning, and monitoring, and allow rapid course correction when things are not going as well as expected.

The art of successfully creating a coaching culture is of course around helping people to develop their coaching skills and competencies. To this degree there is the need to teach the principles of coaching, to ensure that people have the opportunity to practice their coaching, that they get proper feedback and supervision, and that they continuously improve their competencies.

Once the key objectives are clear, then strong support and commitment will be needed from the top of the organization to be the active sponsors. It is also critical that these senior leaders are able, early on, to role model the Leading with Coaching that they expect from others.

These sponsors will need to set the expectation as to what this new path will require in terms of learning, time commitment, qualification, and mindset in order for it to produce the required return on investment. This will need to be laid out, normally many times over, in order to prepare an organization to make the changes that will be needed to succeed.

Formation: The Combination of Training and Practice

In order to instill a coaching culture, there are two phases that need to be formed—coaching skills training and coaching skills practice.

In the initial stage, the introduction of the philosophy of coaching is needed as well as training on the key coaching approaches an organization wants to adopt. This will require clarity on the key coaching methodologies that the training program will promote as the fundamental skills requirements of those participating.

Once people are trained in the coaching basics to be adopted, the approach to practice needs to be carefully considered.

A few years ago, we saw a major corporation trying to implement a very good coaching training program. Because they knew that sponsorship from the top was vital, they decided to implement it with their top 150 leaders in the first instance. However, the program ultimately failed, and it suffered considerable reputational damage, because the 150 top leaders were expected to practice on each other. The program planners had completely underestimated the sense of competition and one-upmanship that existed within this group of senior executives and how this longstanding sense of mistrust would derail the creation of a coaching culture with this cohort of senior people. This resulted in breaches of confidentiality, lowering of trust, and personal agendas being given precedent over good coaching practice as the competition between these leaders sabotaged the intended benefits. The moral of this story is that the coaches, when in the practice phase, need careful and considered curation and monitoring to ensure the system is healthy and is achieving the required organizational outcomes.

There is also a need to consider how to monitor participation levels and competency levels and to make clear what the consequences will be if these are not achieved.

When implemented well, coaching programs designed to create a coaching culture can achieve true magic by fostering trust and cross-functional understanding through the coaching relationships they foster, across different levels within an organization.

Where you have a marketer being coached by a finance person, both get real insight into the value that each function brings and the challenges that can occur between the different functions. We recently saw a good example of this. Every time this particular company had a profit challenge, the finance department suggested that the quick fix to this would be to cut advertising and promotion budgets as an easy and low consequence way of cutting costs. Each time this happened, the marketing department would push back since the consequences are being underestimated by the finance department and the friction cycle would restart between the two departments. However, through the cross-functional coaching that happened as a result of the implementation of the coaching culture program, the shared understanding that was created was used to find ways to help each other to both protect profit and protect the company's brands and brand performance such that a win-win situation was achieved.

This is just one example of how coaching cultures can move the performance needle and help develop the trust and thinking partnerships that turn problems into collective problem-solving.

We advocate, as a means to measure return on investment as well as engagement, that there be a certification process at the end of the formation period for all participants.

We have also observed that well-implemented coaching programs designed to create coaching cultures are highly appreciated by participants. Not only do they enjoy the learning and the practice of a new leadership and interpersonal skill at work, but perhaps more importantly, they see how these skills can be used with their family members and friends. Unlike many training programs, participants often become quickly convinced by both the professional and personal benefits of this learning. This is also often reflected in improved employee engagement scores.

Measuring the success of this type of initiative is never easy and not always as scientific as some might want, so it takes organizational commitment to thinking through how to measure success and then to actually do so. This is often a combination of gathering feedback, empirical case studies and stories, as well as tracking things like the number of coaching sessions that take place, the weight that such programs can have on improving employee engagement, and other more scientific measurements.

Best Practices from Real-Life Businesses to Create a Coaching Culture

By Rainer Schmitz, Executive Coach, Head of The Preston Associates Asia

In recent years you might have heard more about coaching cultures in companies, but the term *coaching culture* might create some irritation. Is it another "flavor of the month" in leadership development? A better way to

(continued)

(continued)

describe it: *shaping your company's culture by using a coaching style in your daily leadership interactions.*

I discovered the "secrets" of coaching 20 years ago when I was still an HR manager, and I became an active advocate. We invested serious money to roll-out a "Manager as Coach" program, we trained all senior leaders and middle managers using coaching frameworks as part of their leadership tools. We reached a great momentum, but at some stage I was rightfully asked: what is our ROI? I was surprised by the question, as the answer seemed logical, but it was not that easy to answer. We analyzed the data we had and we came back with a significant payback: we lowered the employee turnover rate below market average (a savings of US$5M; a conservative calculation), we increased engagement, and we were selected as a Top Employer in Beijing.

This was due to the fact that leaders who use coaching as part of their management style are able to directly influence engagement and will therefore create a higher employee morale and job satisfaction. This is confirmed in the data from the Center for Creative Leadership research,[1] where they conclude that coaching is expected to impact a broad range of intangible benefits, including:

- Employee engagement (+67%), followed closely by increased job satisfaction and morale (+62%).
- Increasing collaboration and teamwork (both +58%).

Leaders in a transformation context benefited from breaking down silos as an important part of the transition. Coaching positively impacting collaboration and teamwork contributed to this transformation.

So, if you want results like these in your organization, how should you go about it? Based on my experience coaching and leading large, global HR organizations at Mondelez and Bacardi, you will need to focus on five key areas to succeed in embedding a holistic coaching road map with impact:

1. Strategic alignment
2. Building the coaching muscle
3. Role modeling
4. Full integration into systems and processes
5. Reinforcement and tracking

1. Strategic Alignment

"In the future, people who are not coaches will not be promoted. Managers who are coaches will be the norm."
—*Jack Welsh, Former Chairman and CEO of GE*

Imagine the power of Jack Welsh's statement for embedding coaching in an organization. To drive coaching into the DNA of the organization, it needs strong commitment from senior leadership, to turn coaching into a strategic, systematic, and longer-term investment, intrinsically connected to your business and leadership strategy.

2. Building the Coaching Muscle

No muscles without good workout. The investment into building capabilities for leaders to be able to coach needs practice and sweat. Coaching is a skill and therefore flight hours

(*continued*)

(continued)

in real-life business situations is essential until it becomes second nature at all levels. The more comfortable leaders are with the practice and coaching muscle, the better they will be at identifying the right moment to use these skills, and when other styles are more appropriate.

3. Role Modeling

The best bosses I had were constructive and honest in their feedback, they were authentic, had regular performance and development discussions, coached, recognized achievements, had a strong business sense, and were fair in their assessment. They role modeled a certain culture that impacted how I lead my teams.

Senior leaders as role models will help to create the coaching momentum. Great leaders use different leadership styles appropriately—coaching being one of them, done in an authentic way. These role models can be your best ambassadors for the power of coaching integrated naturally in how you lead, so make sure you leverage their first-hand testimonials to share their own experience and learning.

4. Full Integration into Business Processes and Systems

Picture this situation: the room is full of senior executives, the business is behind expectations, but the atmosphere is relaxed. The head of the organization, recognized for being very adept at coaching and mentoring, leads the meeting via powerful questions, such as: "What do you think is possible to improve our business results? How can I/we help you to improve? What can we/you do differently? What is your recommendation? What is getting in our way? I appreciate your perspective: this is what I heard you say. . . ."

This is what coaching looks like when it's integrated in daily business interactions. Coaching becomes a mindset. To get to this stage, coaching needs to be implemented into the key business and people systems and processes: in strategic business reviews, during performance and development reviews, in succession planning, leadership development programs, and even rewards and recognition.

5. Reinforcement and Tracking

We have all participated in trainings and workshops. What happened with all the material? What happened with all the knowledge? Usually in only four weeks most of the content disappears from our memory.

To effectively reinforce and track a coaching program, it is essential to establish clear objectives and measurable outcomes from the outset. Regular check-ins and feedback sessions should be scheduled to assess progress and address any challenges. Make sure you also leverage tools like performance metrics, surveys, and self-assessments to track results and impact over time. Encouraging participants to document their reflections and achievements can also foster a sense of accountability. Additionally, creating a support network of peers and mentors within the organization can help sustain momentum. Finally, sharing success stories and data-driven insights with stakeholders reinforces the value of coaching and drives continuous improvement.

(continued)

(*continued*)

In summary, good coaching moves the needle and creates an impact. Leaders who use coaching as part of their leadership style influence engagement and therefore create higher employee morale and job satisfaction, ultimately driving business performance.

The Decision to Go Internal or External

Another decision to be made is whether to implement this type of initiative using internal or external resources. The good news is that this is not a binary choice, as you can successfully combine both approaches for maximum impact.

When deciding between using internal or external coaches for a coaching program, there are several factors to consider. The next sections break down the pros and cons of each approach.

Internal Coaches

Pros:

- **Shorthand to culture:** They understand the company culture, values, and internal dynamics, which allows them to tailor their coaching to the specific context of the organization.

- **Accessibility:** It might be simpler to connect for ongoing support and follow-up, schedule sessions, and seek ad hoc guidance.

- **Cost-effective:** Depending on the size of the organization, internal resources can be cost-effective as they don't charge the fees associated with external coaches.

- **Aligned objectives:** Internal coaches are typically more aware of the organization's objectives and can ensure that the coaching goals are closely tied to company priorities.

Cons:

- **Potential conflicts of interest:** They may have existing relationships with coachees or other stakeholders, leading to potential conflicts of interest if confidentiality is not carefully kept.
- **Perceived bias:** Internal coaches may be perceived as biased or less confidential, which can limit the openness of coachees during sessions.
- **Limited perspective:** Internal coaches may lack an external viewpoint, which can sometimes limit their ability to challenge the status quo or introduce new ideas and approaches.
- **Capacity constraints:** Internal coaches tend to have additional responsibilities within the organization, limiting the time and energy they can dedicate to coaching.

External Coaches

Pros:

- **Objectivity:** External coaches bring an impartial perspective, which can foster greater openness and honesty in coaching sessions. Coachees may feel more comfortable discussing sensitive issues.
- **Diverse expertise:** Experienced external coaches bring a wealth of experience from various industries and organizations, offering fresh insights and best practices to cross-fertilize perspectives and plans.

- **Confidentiality:** External coaches who are certified and practice professionally are bound to the code of ethics of the ICF (International Coaching Federation), which is strict and helps protect a higher level of confidentiality, leading to more candid conversations, especially when dealing with complex, personal, or sensitive issues.

- **Flexibility and focus:** They are fully dedicated to the coaching relationship, without the distraction of other internal responsibilities, allowing them to focus entirely on the development of the coachee.

Cons:

- **Higher costs:** External coaching can be more expensive, particularly if a large number of employees are involved or long-term engagements are required. Therefore, building the appropriate program design using metrics and tracking can help ensure visibility of your ROI.

- **Gradual understanding of your context:** It may take time to understand the company's unique culture and internal dynamics.

- **Alignment gaps:** External coaches may not be as familiar or up to speed with the organization's specific goals and values, requiring more effort to ensure that coaching objectives support overall business objectives.

In essence, choosing between internal and external coaches depends on the specific needs of your organization, the goals of the coaching program, and the nature of the issues being addressed. Some organizations may benefit from a hybrid approach, combining the strengths of internal and external coaching resources.

Case Study: Leading Beyond Your Function to Build a Robust Leadership Coaching Culture That Still Moves the Needle, 10 Years In

By Julie Stokes, O.B.E. (Order of the British Empire)

The board directors of a division of a fast-moving consumer company in the UK agreed that to deliver their growth ambitions they urgently needed a group of senior leaders to be more accountable—"to step up." We challenged the board to be clearer on what specifically stepping up really meant for these leaders. A key requirement was the ability to better lead the business to achieve its ambitions through the adoption of a coaching capability to enhance their leadership skills. They selected 25 of these leaders to participate and pass a program called Advanced Coaching Expertise (ACE), aimed at building leadership capability and trust through learning and practicing coaching skills for this Senior Leadership Group (SLG).

The ACE program initially involved a training element, so everyone understood how coaching competencies formed part of their leadership toolkit. All 25 members of the SLG were then allocated three coachees. These comprised a direct report, a peer, and the golden opportunity to coach someone from another function, such that if you worked in marketing, you would coach someone, say, from finance. The 75 coaching journeys created a web of thinking partnerships within the business, working on real-life business and performance challenges. The cross-functional coaching

(continued)

(continued)

of peers and talented junior employees significantly reduced the sense of silos and fractures so frequently observed when a company is growing fast.

During the year, the program brought together small groups of the SLG to discuss their experience of coaching. Confidential supervision with qualified external coaches was put in place so participants felt able to talk openly about their challenges. The experience of participants learning, solving problems, and celebrating successes together bonded a normally competitive peer group that was often eager for attention from the board. Instead, the SLG emerged as a highly collaborative success driver within the business. The usual stereotyping of different functions was markedly reduced by exposure to coaching and learning what it was really like to work in supply chain, finance, HR, sales, and all the other different functions. The board welcomed the increased challenge and accountability from their more confident community of senior leaders who were now acting as a unit, in sync.

At the end of the program's first year (which was timed to dovetail with end-of year-reviews), all 25 participants were required to demonstrate coaching competency in a live session observed by a coaching assessor. The commitment of the senior leadership to the critical need to pass this stage successfully gave the accreditation process a sharper edge and delivered a strong message about the importance of Leading through Coaching and that it was mandatory. And yet even with this pressure of performance expectation, participants described ACE as stretching and fun.

The ACE end-of-year graduation also saw many coachees share their experience of being listened to and challenged; it was a moment of great pride for the board, who had supported an ambitious and timely intervention. The following year the board requested their own ACE program. They too wanted to be leadership role models. It is often harder for C-Suite members to openly admit that they want to develop leadership skills, but they had the courage and vulnerability to go for it.

ACE coaches in the business continued to coach cross-functionally and they used coaching in all their one-to-ones with their direct reports.

The company was a finalist in a national award, which judged the innovative organizational design to be pivotal in creating a strong leadership culture during a time of double-digit growth. A 10-year follow-up has since shown people rating the intervention as the "best career development I have ever done."

"Leaders don't create followers, they create more leaders. The best leaders are coaches who empower others to achieve their full potential."

—*Tom Peters, Management Guru and Author*

25

A Look into the Future: What Leaders Need to Be Future-Fit

If you are a leader in the business world or in an organization of any kind, it will come as no surprise to you that the world is changing and evolving at a rapid pace: if it feels like it's happening faster than ever, you are not wrong.

According to the World Economic Forum in its 2020 Global Risks Report, "we are living in a time of unprecedented change, where the speed of technological innovation, climate change, and geopolitical shifts are reshaping the global landscape faster than at any other point in history."[1]

The pace of change is also accelerating due to demographic shifts and new business models that are disrupting industries and redefining the nature of work, as described by the *Harvard Business Review* in its *Agile at Scale*.[2]

In this context, the need to upskill and reskill teams and ourselves is becoming an imperative to stay relevant and competitive. Recent research from McKinsey in "The Future of Work"[3] showed that the half-life of skills is shortening, requiring constant learning and adaptation.

In addition, the longevity of business strategies is getting shorter every cycle. The pace of change has accelerated to such a degree that leaders must constantly reevaluate and adapt their strategies. Organizations need to be more agile and resilient than ever before, as shared by Deloitte Insights in their "Thriving in the Age of Disruption: Building Resilient Organizations".[4]

The world is indeed changing at an unprecedented rate, affecting how businesses operate and how leaders must respond to remain relevant and successful.

Therefore, this chapter shares what we view as the top four leadership skills that will be most valuable in the future, and how coaching can help you harness their power to build an edge to your work as a leader and with your teams.

Emotional Intelligence (EI)

Even though this is not a new concept, as it was made popular especially by the groundbreaking work of Daniel Goleman since the publication of his book *Emotional Intelligence: Why It*

Can Matter More Than IQ[5] in 1995, emotional intelligence will be even more important in a future in which human interactions will be more transactional, mediated by technology, and less frequent.

In a nutshell, emotional intelligence (EI) is the ability to recognize, understand, manage, and influence one's own emotions and the emotions of others. It involves skills such as self-awareness, empathy, emotional regulation, and effective communication, which are crucial for building strong relationships and making thoughtful decisions.

Your ability to "read the room" and connect genuinely will be even more critical for fostering strong relationships, having effective communication, and creating a positive work environment.

In times of rapid change and transformation, leaders with high emotional intelligence can maintain composure and provide clear, empathetic communication. This helps to reassure stakeholders, maintain trust, and guide the organization through adversity. Their ability to remain calm and focused under pressure is essential for making sound decisions and leading teams through times of change.

Additionally, leaders with a strong EI will be better at adapting faster, because they can create an environment where team members feel safe to express their ideas without fear of judgment or criticism. This psychological safety is crucial for fostering innovation, as it encourages people to take risks and think creatively, leading to more innovative solutions and competitive advantages.

As mentioned in a previous chapter, coaching can help develop all four key areas of emotional intelligence, as visualized in the summary graph in Figure 25.1.

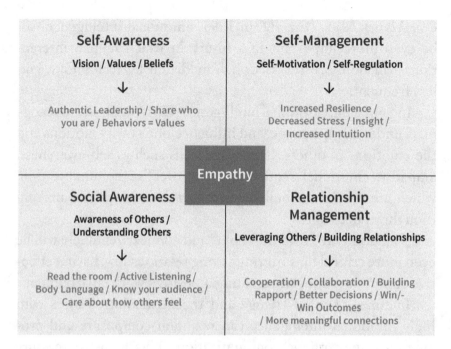

FIGURE 25.1 EI Components and Benefits of Coaching

Digital Literacy and Technological Fluency

As a counterbalance to EI, it's undeniable that leaders, even at the most senior levels, will need to become extremely comfortable and adept at leveraging technology to drive innovation and performance. Understanding digital tools, data analytics, and AI will be crucial for making informed decisions in a tech-driven world. This does not mean that every CEO will need to learn how to code, but it does require that at a minimum, senior leaders understand the power of transformative technologies, and that they create the right conditions to unleash its power in a well-orchestrated manner.

There are many nay-sayers that fear or downplay the impact that technology will have in every aspect of our lives. This ostrich approach of closing our eyes to the inevitable will only make organizations and teams more vulnerable, and they risk losing relevance and competitiveness if they don't jump on the train while they still can.

The key for leaders to embrace technology is to approach it through the lens of a *growth mindset*, defined by psychologist Carol Dweck[6] as the belief that abilities and intelligence can be developed through dedication, effort, and learning. This mindset will be crucial for leaders who aim to embrace technology, as it encourages a positive and proactive approach to learning, adaptation, and innovation. Coaching can be the key enabler to help leaders approach this warp-speed transformation with a sense of openness and possibilities, instead of the resistance that can appear if people tackle these challenges through the lens of a fixed mindset.

Leaders can embrace technology by adopting a proactive and strategic approach, ensuring that they leverage technological advancements to drive innovation, efficiency, and competitive advantage within their organizations. Coaching will play a critical role in this process by helping leaders navigate the complexities of technology adoption, enhance their digital literacy, and align technological initiatives with their organizational goals and values.

The following table shows how leaders can embrace technology and the role that you as a leader-coach can play.

Development Area	How Coaching Can Help
Developing digital literacy through continuous learning: understanding the basics of AI, data analytics, and emerging technologies.	Coach your team to identify their digital literacy gaps and create personalized learning plans to build these skills effectively.
Create hands-on experience opportunities, experimenting with digital tools and platforms to gain first-hand experience and insights.	Build confidence by overcoming apprehension or resistance, fostering a mindset of curiosity and openness.

(*continued*)

(continued)

Development Area	How Coaching Can Help
Build a digital vision: Integrate technology into your strategic vision, identifying how digital tools can be used to achieve long-term business goals, improve customer experience, and streamline operations.	**Change Management**: Coaching provides support in managing the human side of digital transformation, helping leaders effectively communicate the vision, overcome resistance, and engage employees in the change process.
Create strategic alignment: Link technology initiatives with the overall business strategy, ensuring that digital transformation efforts are purposeful and impactful.	**Encouraging Creativity:** Coach your team to cultivate an innovative mindset, allowing them to take calculated risks and explore new technological possibilities.
Leading remote and hybrid teams: Invest in the right technology tools to support remote and hybrid work, ensuring that teams remain productive, engaged, and connected.	**Balancing Technology and Human Connection:** Coaching can guide leaders in balancing the use of technology with maintaining strong human connections, ensuring that virtual work does not lead to isolation or disengagement.
Get good at virtual leadership, adapting your leadership style to manage remote teams effectively, focusing on clear communication, trust-building, and performance management in a virtual environment.	As a leader-coach, you can help develop key skills needed to lead remote and hybrid teams, such as virtual communication, remote team building, and digital empathy.
Building resilience in a tech-driven world by galvanizing infrastructures and people: This includes investing in IT systems that can withstand disruptions to ensure business continuity, but also spending quality time developing the conditions for resilient teams that are capable to hold the tension between the different competing forces that they will have to mediate in a fast-changing environment.	**Developing emotional resilience** by helping your team navigate the stress and uncertainty that often accompany rapid technological change. Coaches can also help deepen self-awareness as a key component of resilience, as it allows individuals to recognize their strengths, weaknesses, emotional triggers, and stress responses. You can coach your team with reflective exercises and feedback to help them gain deeper insights into themselves, better manage their reactions to stress, and identify areas for personal growth, which contributes to greater resilience.

Adaptability and Agility

The ability to adapt quickly to changing circumstances and pivot strategies as needed is vital in a world characterized by rapid change and uncertainty. Agile leaders can help their organizations stay resilient and competitive; they can pivot strategies, adjust goals, and reallocate resources swiftly in response to new challenges or opportunities.

Agile leaders are also more resilient: in a volatile environment, unforeseen disruptions—such as economic downturns, natural disasters, or supply chain disruptions—can occur at any time. Adaptable leaders can respond to these crises with flexibility, ensuring their organizations remain resilient and capable of bouncing back.

Coaching can help develop adaptability and agility by focusing on mindset shifts, skill development, and practical strategies. As a leader-coach, you can help your team become more agile and adaptable through:

- **Cultivating a growth mindset,** to view challenges as opportunities for learning and growth rather than threats. Coaching can help leaders become more comfortable with uncertainty and change, fostering a willingness to experiment and take calculated risks.

- **Improving decision-making skills by building practice and muscle** to make quick, calculated, and informed decisions with frameworks that allow them to assess risks, consider multiple perspectives, and make timely decisions even with incomplete information. As a good leader-coach, you can encourage your team to trust their instincts while also relying on data and feedback, balancing intuition with analysis in decision-making processes.

- **Strengthening trust and collaboration in your teams,** by empowering them to make more decisions at a lower level, versus escalating into bottlenecks that will slow down the pace of the organization. Trust is built through frequent communication and consistent collaboration, especially when managing change and aligning teams with new directions. As a leader-coach, you can help your team refine their communication skills, ensuring that they can clearly articulate vision, strategy, and expectations during times of change. Your coaching can also enhance collaboration skills, enabling leaders to work effectively with diverse teams and build consensus quickly when adapting to new situations.

• **Encouraging flexibility in their leadership style** by recognizing when and how to adapt their leadership style to suit different situations. This flexibility is key to agility, as different challenges will require different approaches, from directive leadership during a crisis to a more democratic style when fostering innovation. Through your coaching, you can help your team grow in self-awareness, understanding their own leadership strengths and areas for improvement, to become more versatile and adaptable in their approach.

Cultural Competence

In our view, this is the next-level evolution of DEI (Diversity, Equity, and Inclusion) through a broader and more holistic lens. In a globalized world, leaders must be able to work effectively across diverse cultures and create inclusive environments that leverage the strengths of a diverse workforce.

Today, executives need to lead people of all ages, races, sexual identities, religions, geographies, and abilities, and in the future this trend will become even more pronounced, with a workforce that for the first time will include six generations, from Boomers to Gen Z, under the same roof.

Cultural competence requires an advanced ability to understand, appreciate, and interact effectively with people from different cultures, backgrounds, and experiences. It involves recognizing and respecting cultural differences, understanding the impact of culture on behavior and communication, and being able to adapt one's approach in a culturally sensitive way.

Leaders who are culturally competent will need to be adept at navigating the core aspects that make up our characteristics, as reflected in the "Identity Wheel" shown in Figure 25.2.

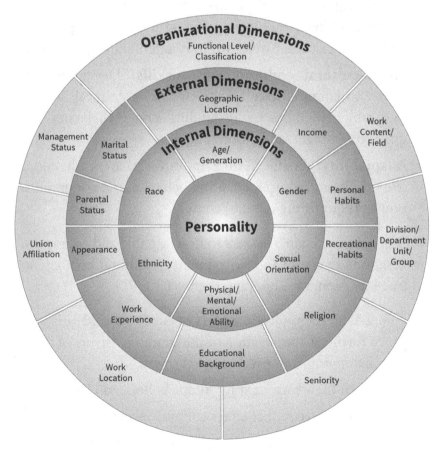

FIGURE 25.2 Identity Wheel.

Source: adapted from *Gardenswartz and Rowe, Diverse Teams at Work: Capitalizing on the Power of Diversity* (2003)

In order to become culturally competent, future-fit leaders will need to develop:

- **Self-awareness:** Understanding one's own cultural background, biases, and assumptions, and how these influence interactions with others.

- **Openness, curiosity, and humility:** Demonstrating a willingness to learn from others, being open to different perspectives, and showing respect for cultural differences.

- **Knowledge of other cultures:** By actively becoming students of different cultures, including their values, practices, and communication styles without judgment or prejudice.

- **Cross-cultural communication skills:** Developing the ability to communicate effectively across cultural boundaries, which includes understanding non-verbal cues, language differences, and cultural norms.

- **Adaptability:** Being flexible in interactions with people from different cultures, adapting behavior and communication styles to fit the cultural context.

Coaching can enable leaders to have capable and courageous conversations to create an environment of cultural competence and true inclusion, by equipping them to:

- Understand the multiple aspects of culture and identity, and gain a nuanced appreciation of the essential drivers of inclusion, belonging, and psychological safety.

- Reflect on their own existing filters, beliefs, and habits.

- Explore out-of-comfort zones and unconscious biases.

- Learn best practices to create an environment of true inclusion and belonging.

- Practice courageous conversations in a safe environment, with non-judgmental guidance and feedback.

- Identify key desired shifts, areas of growth, and opportunities to practice new leadership behaviors to create a truly inclusive environment.

- Create personal commitments to action, including accountability plans.

Cultural competence is critical for effective leadership and collaboration in today's globalized world. Coaching can play a vital role in developing cultural competence by enhancing self-awareness, building knowledge of other cultures, developing cross-cultural communication skills, encouraging openness and curiosity, promoting adaptability, and strengthening leadership in diverse environments. Through coaching, individuals can become more culturally competent, enabling them to navigate cultural differences with confidence and respect.

Case Study: Cultural Competence in Real Life

By Catherine Eidens, Executive Coach, Asia
  Names and details have been altered for confidentiality purposes.

Background

This case study focuses on Bonnie, a general manager reporting to the newly appointed CFO, Erik. Erik, from a Nordic culture, leads a diverse team in Hong Kong, with members predominantly from various Asian backgrounds. Bonnie, a homegrown talent, heads two-thirds of Erik's finance team. Known for her cooperative, empathetic nature and quick problem-solving skills, she efficiently leads her team to deliver results.

(continued)

(continued)

Bonnie was promoted to the GM position two years ago, recognized for her people skills by Erik's predecessor. With the appointment of the new CFO, Bonnie senses a need for change as she struggles to meet Erik's expectations.

Challenge

Erik values open dialogue, transparency, and directness in communication, encouraging equality and consensus in decision-making. He believes in including everyone's opinions.

Bonnie, however, prioritizes harmony and respect for authority. She prefers one-on-one communication with Erik for decision-making, finding it more respectful and professional than expressing contradictory ideas in team meetings.

Known for her pragmatic approach and quick problem-solving skills, Bonnie focuses on efficient outcomes. She finds lengthy discussions in meetings counterproductive and often remains quiet during team discussions. Erik perceives Bonnie's quietness as low engagement and reluctance to share opinions openly. This perception has led him to question her performance and suitability for leading a large team.

Action

Erik decided to support Bonnie with coaching to enhance her leadership and cultural competence. He encouraged her to voice her thoughts openly, even if it contradicted her cultural upbringing practices. He also motivated her to foster a culture of open communication within her team, allowing collaborative ideas to emerge.

The coaching focused on three main areas:

- **Self and cultural differences awareness**: Bonnie began by building a strong understanding of the different cultural competencies required for successful leadership in her role, emphasizing a more participative and contributive approach. She developed a robust self-awareness of her beliefs, values, strengths, leadership principles, and aspirations.

- **Understanding the organizational culture**: Bonnie evaluated her CFO and the current organizational culture and context, considering how to successfully manage her team through change. Bonnie knows that by facilitating cultural understanding within her team, they will have a better chance of meeting Erik's and the company's expectations, as her team is rather monocultural with members being from Hong Kong.

- **Managing cultural and leadership differences**: Bonnie aimed to boost trust and safety, and encourage herself and her team to adopt a new way of active listening and sharing without crossing cultural respect and boundaries. She guided her team to appreciate the benefits of adopting a new leadership culture and approaches. By valuing her team's diverse thought processes consistently, she was able to further empower them.

During their coaching sessions, they focused on shifting perspectives and using some of the coaching

(*continued*)

(*continued*)

frameworks in this book to translate mindset changes into actionable steps:

- Through the authentic leadership frameworks, Bonnie recognized that her upbringing principles, beliefs, and cultural background were essential components of her past success. However, she also realized that they might have limited her and her team's potential for future success in the organizational contexts.

- Mindset transformation. Bonnie embraced the thinking of the performance equation ($P = C \times A^2$), changing the narrative of her challenge from cultural differences to recognizing diversity as a source of strengths.

- Bonnie honed her C.A.L.M. listening skills to understand the challenges and emotions faced by her team and Erik. Additionally, she delved into Trilogy Questions—dedicating enough time to deconstruct questions such as What do I want? and How do Erik and the team measure success in this situation? She also explored ways to enhance communication in all directions and identified her success partners. Her team culture value of leading by example became evident as she actively listened more and clarified the definition of success. They also adopted more of these practices.

Outcome

Building on further understanding of diversity in thinking, working principles and styles, Bonnie consistently demonstrated empathy without judgment and utilized her cross-cultural understanding with her team. Subsequently, she earned a promotion to a director position after a year of coaching.

A Last Reflection: Leading in a World Where Certainty Is Over

In a VUCA world that's in a constant state of change and transformation, leaders can no longer expect, and even less promise, certainty. Certainty is over, and the next best thing is clarity.

The good news for you as a leader-coach is that clarity is something you can **_create_**. Every step and every framework in this book has been built to help you construct, create, and co-create clarity as part of your leadership skills, to coach your teams into a state of clarity and alignment.

From the Trilogy Questions that can help you go from the WHAT to the HOW, WHO, and WHEN, to the performance equation, and courageous conversations—these frameworks are purposely simple and practical because we believe that clarity and simplicity go hand in hand.

However, in times of change and turbulence, it's easy to get lost, so to help you regain a sense of clarity, consider these simple self-reflection prompts. These prompts are designed to help you explore your leadership approach and business strategy more deeply, identifying areas where greater clarity can lead to more effective action and better outcomes.

Exercise: Regaining Clarity

Self-reflection is a powerful tool for gaining clarity, especially in business and leadership. Here are some essential prompts designed to help you reflect on your business and leadership practices, with the goal of creating greater clarity:

- What is the core purpose of my leadership role? How clearly have I communicated this purpose to my team?

(continued)

(continued)

- What are the most important goals for my business right now? How clear are they to me and my team?

- Are my priorities aligned with these goals, or are there conflicting demands that need to be addressed?

- What criteria am I using to determine what is most important? Are these criteria still relevant?

- How does my current business strategy align with my long-term vision? Is there anything that needs to be adjusted?

- What are the biggest challenges facing my business or leadership today? What is unclear about how to address them?

- What obstacles are preventing me from making clear decisions? Are these internal (mindset, emotions) or external (resources, market conditions)?

- What impact do I want to have on my team and organization? How clearly am I achieving that impact?

- How effectively am I communicating with my team? Are there any areas where clarity is lacking?

- How well does my team understand their roles, responsibilities, and the bigger picture? What can I do to enhance their clarity?

- What is my decision-making process, and how effective is it in creating clarity for myself and others?

- What decisions have I been avoiding? What clarity do I need to move forward with them?

- Where do I need to take more risks? Where do I need to de-risk?

- What legacy do I want to leave as a leader? How does that influence my decisions today?

- In what areas do I feel most confident as a leader, and where do I feel uncertain or unclear?

- Looking back at the past year, what were the most significant moments of clarity I experienced? What prompted them?

- What lessons have I learned from times when clarity was lacking? How can I apply those lessons moving forward?

- How can I create a regular practice of reflection, to create clarity and ensure continuous growth in my business and leadership?

"The biggest risk is not taking any risk. In a world that is changing really quickly, the only strategy that is guaranteed to fail is not taking risks."

—Mark Zuckerberg, Founder/Creator of Facebook

26

Artificial Intelligence: The Single Most Powerful Force Shaping the Future

As a business leader, you are familiar with the groundbreaking power that AI will have, as it is set to transform the world in profound ways over the next decades, impacting nearly every aspect of our lives. One of the most significant changes will be the personalization of technology. Imagine a future where your devices—like your phone, computer, or even your home—know you so well that they can anticipate your needs before you even voice them. AI will make this possible by learning your habits, preferences, and routines, allowing your technology to offer suggestions, reminders, and solutions that are tailored specifically to you. This will create a more seamless and intuitive interaction with the technology around you, making everyday tasks easier and more efficient.

In healthcare, AI will revolutionize how we diagnose and treat diseases. By analyzing vast amounts of medical data, AI will help doctors identify health issues earlier and more accurately than ever before. This could lead to more personalized treatments and better patient outcomes, potentially even preventing diseases before symptoms arise. The impact on healthcare could be life-changing, with AI enabling quicker diagnoses and more effective therapies, ultimately leading to longer and healthier lives.

Transportation will also undergo a dramatic shift as AI-powered self-driving cars become more common. These vehicles will be able to navigate roads more safely than human drivers, reducing accidents caused by human error. In addition to making our roads safer, self-driving cars will also make transportation more efficient, cutting down on traffic congestion and making commutes faster and more pleasant.

In cities, AI will manage traffic systems, energy use, and public transportation more efficiently, leading to smarter, more sustainable urban environments. AI could reduce pollution, conserve energy, and make city living more convenient and enjoyable.

Creatively, AI will collaborate with humans to produce art, music, and literature, opening new frontiers in entertainment and design. This partnership between human creativity and AI's capabilities will lead to innovative forms of expression that blend the best of both worlds.

Finally, AI will play a crucial role in addressing global challenges like climate change, food security, and healthcare crises. By analyzing data and identifying patterns, AI can help develop solutions that might otherwise go unnoticed, making the world more sustainable and safer.

AI is poised to reshape our world in ways that will make life easier, safer, and more personalized. It will revolutionize industries, improve healthcare, transform how we work, and help us tackle some of the biggest challenges we face. While these changes will require us to adapt, they also hold the promise of making the next decade one of the most exciting and transformative periods in history.

The Impact of AI in Business

In terms of organizational impact at large, in our research and day-to-day work with the top 10% of leaders in Fortune 500 companies globally, we have identified five main areas that we believe will be deeply impacted by AI.

Enhanced Decision-Making

In the next five years we anticipate that decisions will go from experience-based, senior-leader-driven to data-driven decisions that can be made at the frontline by lower-level leaders. AI-driven platforms like IBM Watson and Salesforce Einstein are being used by the companies we work with to analyze customer data, market trends, and operational performance. These tools already help leaders make more informed strategic decisions, from product development to customer engagement, in real time and at all levels of the organization, allowing businesses to act in a faster and more agile way.

When AI is adopted broadly, employees up and down the hierarchy will augment their own judgment and intuition with algorithms' recommendations to arrive at better answers than either humans or machines could reach on their own. But for this approach to work, leaders at all levels need to trust the algorithms' suggestions and feel empowered to make decisions— which means abandoning the traditional top-down approach.

Automation and Productivity

Companies like Amazon and Walmart already use AI extensively to optimize their supply chains. AI systems predict demand, manage inventory, and streamline logistics, allowing leaders to focus on strategic initiatives rather than day-to-day operations. McKinsey & Company reports[1] that AI could automate up to 45% of these activities, significantly impacting leadership by shifting focus from operational tasks to strategic growth.

Furthermore, in a recent analysis by PwC in *"Sizing the Prize: What's the Real Value of AI for Your Business,"*[2] the report suggests that AI could contribute up to $15.7 trillion to the global economy by 2030 (more than the current output of China and India combined), with productivity improvements accounting for more than half of this gain.

Talent Management and Reskilling

AI is poised to have a significant impact on the job market, with both positive and negative effects depending on the industry and profession. While AI will automate many routine tasks, leading to job displacement in certain sectors, it will also create new jobs that require advanced technical skills. The challenge will be in reskilling and upskilling workers to meet the demands of these new roles.

There will be a growing need for soft skills such as creativity, emotional intelligence, and critical thinking—skills that are difficult for AI to replicate. Jobs that involve complex problem-solving, human interaction, and strategic decision-making are likely to thrive.

The professions that will benefit from AI include data science and analytics, healthcare (through early diagnosis and personalized medicine), education and training (for personalized instruction and AI-driven curriculums), and manufacturing (through the need for engineers in advanced robotics, machine maintenance, and quality control).

The professions that are likely to be negatively impacted include routine manual labor, clerical and administrative roles, retail and customer service, transportation and logistics, and basic financial services.

AI may exacerbate economic inequality, as workers in high-skill, high-demand jobs (like AI specialists) will see wage growth, while those in automatable roles face unemployment or wage stagnation. Policies and programs aimed at workforce development and education will be essential to mitigate these effects.

AI is expected to create 97 million new jobs by 2025, particularly in areas like data analysis, machine learning, and AI development, while also displacing some existing jobs.

To get ahead of these trends, companies are already implementing initiatives to develop and reskill their talents. For example, AT&T's Workforce 2020 initiative uses AI to identify skills gaps and recommend personalized training programs for employees, helping frontline leaders ensure their workforce is prepared for the future. Amazon has recently launched the Career Choice Program to invest $700 million to upskill 100,000 US employees by 2025. The program offers employees the opportunity to learn new skills and transition into high-demand jobs within or outside of Amazon. The program covers 95% of tuition for courses in high-demand fields like healthcare, IT, and AI trades.

Personalization and Customer Experience

Based on a recent analysis by *Forbes*,[3] this field went from experimental to mainstream in less than five years, as AI is revolutionizing customer experience by enabling hyper-personalization. You already have many AI enabled moments in your daily life, from the Netflix algorithm that recommends what to watch next, to your LinkedIn feed, and your Starbucks seasonal suggestions.

However, these are early days, and AI has enormous untapped power in hyper-personalization. The future will bring (sooner than we think) very concrete new personalized services like AI companions for elderly people that will know their medical history, manage medical appointments, ensure compliance to medication, and will also have a soft-skill set that will include adapting to their conversational style and even playing games. These AI companions will evolve and grow with users over time, leading to entirely new forms of social interaction and emotional support, blending AI with human relationships in unprecedented ways.

Innovation and New Business Models

Chances are that you have already used multiple businesses that are powered by AI, without even noticing: from Uber's back-end that connects drivers with passengers, to the DNA testing service 23andMe, shifting the leadership focus toward integrating AI into core business strategies.

The market size of businesses powered by AI is rapidly growing and has become a significant part of the global economy. According to the analysis from Grand View Research,[4] the global AI market was valued at approximately $400 billion in 2022 and by 2030, the market is projected to reach $1.81 trillion.

In terms of enterprise adoption, as of 2023, 56% of companies have reported using AI in at least one function, such as marketing, finance, or operations. Companies that have successfully integrated AI into their operations have seen significant revenue growth: businesses using AI for sales have reported revenue increases of 5–10% over companies that have not adopted AI.

When it comes to investing in new businesses powered by AI, in 2022, venture capital (VC) investment in AI start-ups exceeded $100 billion, a clear indicator of the industry's growth potential. There are thousands of AI-focused start-ups globally, with notable hubs in the United States, China, and Europe. The number of AI start-ups has been growing exponentially, reflecting the increasing demand for AI-driven solutions across various industries.

The AI-powered business sector is growing rapidly, both in terms of market value and its impact across various industries. The integration of AI into business operations is driving significant economic value, with projections indicating that AI will continue to be a major force in the global economy for years to come.

Then What? The Impact of AI in Leadership

If you have been following the media and general opinion and trends, you know that AI has as many fans as it has detractors. When it comes to the world of business, in the conversations that we are having with the most senior leaders we coach, we are sensing a mixture of excitement about the possibilities of AI to drive and optimize performance, and concern about the consequences of it for people and jobs.

It is still early days to be able to accurately predict the full impact of AI in leadership, but from the existing research from multiple sources, we can already see that AI will significantly impact the future of leadership by shifting the emphasis from "hard" leadership skills to "soft" skills:

- **Hard skills like data processing will be automated.** AI can augment and potentially replace many cognitive aspects of leadership like analyzing data and information. As per a study by the MIT-IBM Watson AI Lab,[5] only 2.5% of jobs have a high proportion of tasks suitable for machine learning, so the role of human intelligence will continue to be crucial in leadership roles.

- **Soft skills like adaptability will become mission-critical.** Leaders will need to be humble about constantly learning from others, open to changing course when needed, able to articulate a clear vision, and deeply engaged with their environment. A *Harvard Business Review* study[6] highlights the rising importance of traits like humility, adaptability, vision, and engagement for effective AI age leadership.

While leadership fundamentals may persist, AI is poised to significantly elevate the importance of leaders' softer, more adaptive capabilities to navigate an era of rapid technological disruption.

Expert Perspective How AI Affects Your Leadership and Coaching Approach: Practically, What Can You Do

By Diana Gan, Executive Coach, Board Member, and Tech Advisor

Artificial Intelligence (AI) has been developing for decades. While certain tech leaders are aware of AI's potential, the deployment of AI did not receive widespread adoption. However, since the release of ChatGPT in November 2022, Generative AI (GenAI), with its ability to generate new content or data points, has taken on an exponential development path. GenAI's adoption rate also surpassed all tech platforms that came before it in record time.

Emerging Business Trends Driven by AI

At the time of writing, a number of key trends are emerging with respect to AI, that beg the question of whether AI can already be an enabler for competitive advantage in business.

Among all its use cases, there is consensus that productivity gains and enhanced user engagement are the low hanging fruits. AI augmenting human decision-making seems to have also gained a foothold. On the other hand, the jury is still out on AI's role in value creation, either in the form of new product or new business models.

At the same time, there are talks that AI will become commoditized much like the penetration of smart phones. If that indeed comes true and AI becomes an integral part of day-to-day work, the choice between investing in AI now in order not to be left behind versus waiting for the cost to come down significantly is not an easy one.

How Should Leaders Think About AI?

Whether one sees the world we live in as a VUCA (volatile, uncertain, complex, ambiguous) world or a BANI (brittle, anxious, non-linear, incomprehensible) world, the challenges that business leaders will need to be cognizant of and incorporate in their decision-making seem to be ever growing. AI, or more broadly disruptive technology, is but one piece of this puzzle.

A useful way to approach strategic thinking for AI is to through the lens of 7 business fundamentals to business fundamentals:

(*continued*)

(*continued*)

1. What part does AI play in my business?

Much like the discussions on the core competencies of an organization, the central questions around AI are: is it a core product, a strategic imperative, part of enterprise risk management, part of new growth through unprecedented hyperscaling, or all of the above? Once leaders have anchored the discussions on a chosen positioning for AI, that will inform how a business case will be framed around AI.

2. What is the tone at the top?

Customers, employees, business partners, and investors would surely wonder, what direction is being set by the board of directors and C-Suite with regards to AI? Boards and C-Suites who take the initiative to frame the narrative upfront and provide a line of one clarity will gain better visibility of stakeholders' response, which in turn informs the definition of success for the organization.

3. How does AI improve the quality of decision-making?

Leaders are ultimately judged by the quality of their decisions. Can leaders maintain curiosity over AI's capability to provide better data and predictive analysis, and to uncover blind spots? Equally importantly, what are the critical mindsets leaders can adopt to ask better questions about AI's capability and be mindful of AI hallucinations?

4. What attitudes do I embrace that will drive high performance through deploying AI?

High performance in business is achieved when attitudes and behaviors are aligned. Myths can be debunked and fears can be allayed through open communication. Leaders who consciously point out "the way we do things around here" when success stories in the deployment of AI are celebrated will find that this effectively drives positive reinforcement of behaviors that lead to wider adoption.

5. What do we stand for as an organization on ethical use of AI?

There are important ethical issues in the deployment of AI—the inherent biases in the datasets that inform the large language models (LLM) on which AI applications run are very real. What awareness can leaders build into their assessment process to call out bias and equity to ensure a more inclusive approach? Who is accountable for ensuring that the agreed approach is carried through to implementation? What level of transparency is shared across the organization and to the public at large?

6. What are the essential guardrails in deploying AI?

Cybersecurity, data privacy, IP protection, capabilities of the vendor, and of course regulations are evergreen topics in the deployment of AI and technology. Compliance may be a drag on innovation, but these are the realities that cannot be ignored and ensure that a firm foundation is in place for advancement in technology.

7. Is my organization ready to embrace AI?

Organizational readiness cuts across the entire fabric of the organization, including organizational structure, culture, talent skill set, talent mindset, transition/transformation readiness. A timely analysis of your readiness helps to put all of these considerations into perspective. In that analysis, ensuring that people are taken care of is a critical underlying

(continued)

(continued)

theme. Investments into upskilling and reskilling, gaining buy-in, designing for collaboration and in some instances, thoughtful alternative placements will be part of the agenda. There is another school of thought where employees are in fact adopting AI faster than the organization itself. How can leaders empower the early adopters to drive change and bring everyone else along?

Whether or not an organization is ready to embrace AI, leaders will no doubt be thinking, how can they ensure that they are not left behind? Embrace lifelong learning and continuous exposure not only for leaders themselves but instilling the same value across the organization sounds like a good starting point.

"In the age of AI characterized by intense disruption and rapid, ambiguous change, we need to rethink the essence of effective leadership. Certain qualities, such as deep domain expertise, decisiveness, authority, and short-term task focus, are losing their cachet, while others, such as humility, adaptability, vision, and constant engagement, are likely to play a key role in more-agile types of leadership."

—*Tomas Chamorro-Premuzic, Michael Wade, and Jennifer Jordan, Harvard Business Review*

27

A Last Word on T.R.U.S.T

In the last few years, as we have coached C-Suite leaders in all sorts of sectors, across multiple geographies and in various geopolitical scenarios, we have become increasingly aware of a serious and developing gap between the relationships that organizations want to create between themselves, customers, stakeholders, partners, and employees and those they actually have. This gap is also a major challenge in respect to regulators, governments, special interest groups, and a plethora of other parties that exist in the orbit of all organizations.

We have also seen that this gap is widening more broadly across the world. People doubt the integrity of politicians, conspiracy theories abound, even scientists with empirical evidence are questioned.

There is a sense that the commercial jungles are haunted by an enemy close to invisible, stealthy and devastating when it strikes. The gap that is widening is of course that of trust—trust in our institutions, political and legal systems, in corporations and their motivation and commitment to doing the right thing for the world and in the interests of those they serve. Trust as an element of leadership credibility is not a new concept. It has always been the case that leaders are expected to be trustworthy. Initially that was toward shareholders and the promises they made to them. This then expanded to a broader set of stakeholders, including consumers, customers, and employees.

And many of the basics of leadership have been successful trust builders—being clear and transparent on the definition of collective success for an organization and the teams expected to deliver that success; codifying and then being a role model and custodian of the behaviors that need to be adopted to foster a successful, productive, and enjoyable work environment where talent can blossom; promoting open and honest dialogue internally within a company and externally with customers and a broad range of other stakeholders. And many other aspects of leadership that we regularly coach our clients on and that you bring to life.

In other words, deliver on the definition of a good leader—someone who absorbs pressure, transmits clarity, and builds the confidence in others that they need to succeed—and it starts to build a foundation of trust.

However, here's the gap. Across the world TRUST is in decline across the board. The 2023 Edelman Trust Barometer[1] showed the worst results on trust in the 23 years that it has been measuring it.

Worse still are these statistics from the PwC Consumer Intelligence Service Series on Trust[2]:

- 87% of executives think that customers highly trust their companies. Yet only 30% of customers say they actually do trust those same companies. So executives overestimate their perception of customer trust in their organizations by a whopping 57%. If leaders and organizations think they are trusted far more than they actually are, they are at risk of making huge mistakes.

- Further, 71% of employees say they will leave a company if it loses their trust.
- And 71% of consumers say they are unlikely to buy if a company loses their trust.

And so we see an increasing alliance between customer experience and employee experience, which not only impacts sales to consumers but also talent attraction and retention strategies.

This leads us to understand that trust is now a tangible asset—it should be part of a company's balance sheet.

When we look at the costs and benefits of low or high trust the evidence is even more stark.

Here are some examples of serious trust breaches since the Global Financial Crisis:

In Finance:

- Of course, the financial crisis itself and the decline in trust in banks and bankers, regulators, and governments
- The Madoff scandal
- And more recently the crisis such as the collapse of Silicon Valley Bank and Signature Bank

Who would have ever believed that a lack of trust—and that's what it was—could lead to the collapse of a 167-year-old institution such as Credit Suisse?

Here are just some examples of the endless scandals that have eroded trust:

- Diesel gate

- The Boeing 737 Max scandal
- The opiate crisis
- The reliability and impartiality of the media
- The geopolitical landscape and people's levels of trust in politicians around the world would seem to be at an all-time low. Political polarization is a symptom of low trust.

The cost in dollars of these is almost incalculable but the cost of society's trust in the world and how it is run is even greater. These trust breaches are just a few of those we might be able to think of over the past two decades.

Yet this is a huge opportunity for business and business leaders. Business can prove itself to be the responsible adult in the trust room if it properly raises leadership expectations and has the courage and moral fiber to be trustworthy and act accordingly as leaders.

There is some sunshine among the trust clouds where we can see the advantages of continuous trust gains, for example in the hyper premium brands for whom trust is at the very foundation of their existence. As frivolous as you might think these to be, they are important barometers. Two examples being Hermes, which recently reported an increase of sales and profits in the 2023 financial year of 29% and 38%, respectively, and LVMH, which reported an increase of 23% and 23%, respectively. Consumers trust these brands, and that is what helps them to grow in even the most difficult market environments.

In finance, we need look no further than Berkshire Hathaway as a beacon of continuous trust gains.

In a messed-up world of war, political turmoil, and extremely low trust in general—these are extremely strong trust indicators for those brands and again prove that trust should be an essential part of leadership thinking and action.

So, what are we supposed to do with all of that?

First, all leaders now have to be clear that, whether they are at the bottom or the top of an organization, they are custodians of trust in their organization and that that is a key part of their leadership responsibilities, mindset, awareness, and obligation to act.

Some companies have appointed a Chief Trust Officer to the top leadership team, although this is not nearly enough as it must be an express requirement for all leaders and all leadership teams at all levels in every organization. Teams across all levels of an organization need to be coached on what this means; they need to understand what they can do to ensure that they are being custodians of, and accelerators of, trust and they need to understand that they are empowered to act to maintain and grow trust.

And they need to understand the key components of T. R. U. S. T. that will help them navigate this trust expectation successfully:

T is for Transparency. Say "I don't know." Quickly and honestly admit to mistakes and move to provide fast and full remedies.

R is for Respect. Act with integrity and proactively show respect for people, opinions, difference, diversity, regulation and "doing the right thing" at all times.

U is for Understanding. Practice active listening to seek understanding on key issues, get quality feedback that allows for measurable improvements in people, services, products, and societal impact—among many other opportunities to leave the world a better place.

S is for Sustainability in all its forms. Act to protect the environment and the climate, act on employee well-being and development, on DE&I, and on societal and geo-political issues. Make sure that your organization in its fullest sense is sustainably successful for the long term. Embrace change. And make no apology for making fair and consistent profit—it is the profits that ultimately make companies sustainable.

T And lastly, the second T is for Truth. Be truthful at all times. And know this—if you are tempted not to be truthful, sooner or later, YOU WILL BE FOUND OUT!

As we say goodbye to you now, we hope that not only will you be the best coach and leader you can possibly be, but also that you will become one of the many of us who will need to reestablish trust for future generations to thrive in the knowledge that we care enough about the future to start to take care of it today.

"Without trust, we don't truly collaborate; we merely coordinate or, at best, cooperate. It is trust that transforms a group of people into a team."

—Stephen Covey, *American Educator and Author*

Notes and References

Chapter 2

1. McKinsey, How To Create an Agile Organization, https://www.mckinsey .com/capabilities/people-and-organizational-performance/our-insights/ how-to-create-an-agile-organization
2. World Economic Forum's The Future of Jobs Report 2023, https://www .weforum.org/publications/the-future-of-jobs-report-2023/
3. McKinsey, How To Create an Agile Organization, https://www.mckinsey .com/capabilities/people-and-organizational-performance/our-insights/ how-to-create-an-agile-organization
4. Gallup Workplace Research, https://www.gallup.com/workplace/285674/ improve-employee-engagement-workplace.aspx.
5. Deloitte's Global Technology Leadership Study and Deloitte's 2020 Digital Transformation Survey.
6. McKinsey Diversity Matters, https://www.mckinsey.com/capabilities/ people-and-organizational-performance/our-insights/why-diversity- matters
7. Boston Consulting Group, https://www.bcg.com/publications/2018/ how-diverse-leadership-teams-boost-innovation

Chapter 3

1. *Harvard Business Review*, "The Impact of Employee Engagement on Performance"
2. McKinsey, The science behind successful transformations, https://www .mckinsey.com/capabilities/people-and-organizational-performance/ our-insights/successful-transformations

3. Edelman Trust Barometer, 2023, https://www.edelman.com/trust/2023/trust-barometer
4. Ethics Resource Center, The Global Business Ethics Survey, 2023.
5. Harvard Business Review, Global Empathy Index, https://hbr.org/2016/12/the-most-and-least-empathetic-companies-2016#:~:text=The%20Empathy%20Index%20seeks%20to,reap%20the%20greatest%20financial%20rewards
6. Catalyst, Empathic Leaders Drive Employee Engagement and Innovation, https://www.catalyst.org/media-release/empathic-leaders-drive-employee-engagement-and-innovation-media-release/
7. McKinsey, For smarter decisions, empower your employees, https://www.mckinsey.com/capabilities/people-and-organizational-performance/our-insights/for-smarter-decisions-empower-your-employees
8. McKinsey, Raising the resilience of your organization, https://www.mckinsey.com/capabilities/people-and-organizational-performance/our-insights/raising-the-resilience-of-your-organization
9. IMD, Resilient leadership: Navigating the pressures of modern working life, https://www.imd.org/research-knowledge/leadership/articles/resilient-leadership-navigating-the-pressures-of-modern-working-life/

Chapter 15

1. Grant, Adam. *Hidden Potential: The Science of Achieving Greater Things*, Ebury Publishing, 2023, ISBN 075-3560-070.

Chapter 24

1. Center for Creative Leadership. *The Value of Coaching Report*, 2019

Chapter 25

1. World Economic Forum. *The Global Risks Report 2020*. Geneva: World Economic Forum. https://www.weforum.org/reports/the-global-risks-report-2020
2. *Harvard Business Review*, "Agile at Scale," https://hbr.org/2018/05/agile-at-scale
3. McKinsey & Company. *The Future of Work*, https://www.mckinsey.com/featured-insights/future-of-work

4. *Deloitte Insights*, "Thriving in the Age of Disruption: Building Resilient Organizations," https://www2.deloitte.com/us/en/insights.html
5. Goleman, Daniel. *Emotional Intelligence: Why It Can Matter More Than IQ*, Bantam Books, 1995, ISBN 978-0553-383-713.
6. Dweck, C. S. *Mindset: The New Psychology of Success.*

Chapter 26

1. McKinsey & Company. *A Future That Works: Automation, Employment, and Productivity* https://www.mckinsey.com/featured-insights/future-of-work/a-future-that-works-automation-employment-and-productivity
2. PwC. (2017). *Sizing the Prize: What's the Real Value of AI for Your Business?* https://www.pwc.com/gx/en/issues/analytics/assets/pwc-ai-analysis-sizing-the-prize-report.pdf
3. *Forbes, How AI Is Revolutionizing Customer Experience*, https://www.forbes.com/sites/forbestechcouncil/2020/07/14/how-ai-is-revolutionizing-customer-experience/?sh=4b7e2a1e4b9e
4. Grand View Research, *Artificial Intelligence Market Size, Share & Trends*, https://www.grandviewresearch.com/industry-analysis/artificial-intelligence-ai-market
5. MIT-IBM Watson AI Lab, *The Future of Work: How New Technologies Are Transforming Tasks*, https://mitibmwatsonailab.mit.edu/research/the-future-of-work/
6. *Harvard Business Review*, "The Best Leaders Are Humble Leaders," https://hbr.org/2018/05/the-best-leaders-are-humble-leaders

Chapter 27

1. Edelman Trust Barometer, 2023, https://www.edelman.com/trust/2023/trust-barometer https://www.edelman.com/trust/2023/trust-barometer
2. PWC Consumer Intelligence Series: *Trusted Tech – The Building Blocks of Consumer Trust*, https://www.pwc.com/us/en/services/consulting/library/consumer-intelligence-series.html

Acknowledgments

First and foremost, we would like to thank our friends and colleagues at The Preston Associates for their contributions to this work, their generous sharing of expertise and knowledge over the many years we have worked and learned together, and for their dedication and professionalism in always putting the interest of clients first.

We would also like to express our gratitude to our clients, who trust us with their most challenging issues, who are always open to learn, and also to share with us how we can serve them even better.

We would never have become Executive Coaches had it not been for the leadership and coaching role modeling that many of our former bosses and leaders shared with us so, though perhaps long forgotten, we would like to thank all those who helped form us as business professionals and ultimately as coaches.

And we would lastly like to thank our publisher, Wiley, for their support, tenacity, encouragement, and enthusiasm for this book. It would never have been born without them. Specifically, we would like to thank Zachary Schisgal and Amanda Pyne from Wiley and our dedicated editor Kezia Endsley.

Index